CHRISTMAS
›AT WAR‹

CHRISTMAS AT WAR

HEARTWARMING TRUE STORIES OF HOW BRITAIN CAME TOGETHER ON THE HOME FRONT

CAROLINE TAGGART

JOHN BLAKE

Published by John Blake Publishing,
2.25, The Plaza,
535 Kings Road,
Chelsea Harbour
London, SW10 0SZ

www.johnblakebooks.com

www.facebook.com/johnblakebooks [f]
twitter.com/jblakebooks [t]

This edition published in 2017

ISBN: 978 1 78606 814 9

British Library Cataloguing-in-Publication Data:

A catalogue record for this book is available from the British Library.

Design by www.envydesign.co.uk

Printed and bound in Great Britain by Clays Ltd, Elcograf S.p.A.

1 3 5 7 9 10 8 6 4 2

Papers used by John Blake Publishing are natural, recyclable products made from
wood grown in sustainable forests. The manufacturing processes conform to the
environmental regulations of the country of origin.

Every reasonable effort has been made to trace copyright-holders of material reproduced
in this book, but if any have been inadvertently overlooked the publishers would be glad
to hear from them.

John Blake Publishing is an imprint of Bonnier Books UK
www.bonnierbooks.co.uk

*For Ann, whose support for this one went way
beyond the call of sisterly duty.*

A NOTE ON MONEY

For those unfamiliar with Britain's coinage in pre-decimalisation days, a pound was divided into twenty shillings and a shilling into twelve pennies. A price of one shilling and sixpence was generally referred to as 'one and six' and written 1/6. Pennies on their own were represented by a d (from the Latin *denarius*), so something that cost sixpence would be written 6d.

Where prices occur in this book I have given a direct equivalent (one shilling = 5p, two and six = 12½p), but this in no way reflects how expensive something seemed, or what people could afford to buy. During the war a comic such as *The Beano* cost 2d (less than 1p), a pint of beer 5d (2p) and a week's ration of groceries under four shillings (20p): ridiculously cheap by today's standards. But a child's weekly pocket money – if it existed at all – would be a few pennies, so spending ten shillings (50p) on a Christmas present would mean saving for months. The diarist Vere Hodgson, whom I have quoted in the text, recorded at one point seeing apples at 1/4 (one shilling and fourpence) a pound – about 6½p – and obviously thought this was outrageous. Bearing in mind that the average annual salary was £200, it *was* outrageous: the average salary in the UK in 2017 was over £27,000, so that equates to paying about £8.77 for three apples. At the other end of the scale, in some parts of the country you could buy a three-bedroomed house for £350, which – using the same calculation – comes out at only £47,250. Try buying a broom cupboard in London for that these days.

CONTENTS

INTRODUCTION

Ask a random group of people in the UK today what Christmas means to them and they'll probably mention – in no particular order – getting together with family, giving and receiving presents, having a couple of weeks off work, eating and drinking too much, spending the afternoon slumped in front of the television. A lot of them will groan, because getting together with family, shopping for food and deciding what to buy as presents are all, frankly, a bit of a nightmare. But they may well admit that they'd miss it if it didn't happen.

During the Second World War, the vast majority of people in Britain didn't have the opportunity to groan about Christmas. With husbands, fathers, brothers and friends away fighting, children evacuated to the country to avoid the danger of bombing, and both men and women working in jobs that gave them very little leave, lengthy family gatherings were not an option. Many people were too poor to spend much on Christmas extravagances, even had there been anything much in the shops to buy; many were worried about the whereabouts of loved ones or grieving over their loss. Some of the lucky ones felt that it was wrong to celebrate when there was so much anxiety and sorrow about. With television broadcasts suspended from 1939 until 1946, the radio, or 'wireless', was the main source of news and entertainment; on Christmas Day, this meant church-like silence for the King's Speech. The King was George VI, whose crippling stutter was made famous for a new generation in the 2010 film starring Colin Firth; an extraordinary number of people who were children during the war recall how painful it was to listen to him struggling with his words. Apart from the wireless, listening to the gramophone, sing-songs round the piano or family games ranging from cards to charades were the best most people could hope for in the way of entertainment.

As for festive food, lots of things that we think of as commonplace were simply unseen from 1939 onwards. Signs reading 'Yes! We Have No Bananas' – the title of a popular song of the 1920s – were often seen outside greengrocers' shops, put there by shopkeepers who were tired of answering the same question over and over again. After the war, many children, seeing these strange bendy items for the first time, tried to eat them skin and all; one eight-year-old boy assumed they were guns. He and his friends may not have recognised exotic fruit, but they knew what guns were and used the bananas to play war games until these strange new toys turned soft and squishy – which can't have taken very long.

The main reason for shortages like this was that, before the war, Britain imported about two-thirds of its food. This made the country immensely vulnerable to anything that interfered with supplies. From the moment hostilities started, German U-boats in the Atlantic targeted merchant ships coming from North America and elsewhere, hoping, effectively, to starve Britain out.

Rationing – a complicated system involving both coupons and points – of food and of lots of other things was introduced with the praiseworthy aim of eking out limited supplies and distributing them fairly to everyone. Understandably enough, the troops came first: civilians had to make sacrifices so that the men on the front line could carry on fighting. The government also encouraged people to eat healthily – a strong, well-fed nation would be better able to fight (and win) the war. Many, particularly the urban poor, had more nutritious diets than ever before as they were forced to cut down on fatty and sugary foods, and fill the gaps with vegetables. But although many in rural areas don't remember going hungry, many in the cities did. There simply wasn't enough to go round.

It goes without saying that fighting a war costs money. Another reason for shortages was a massive export drive – the more goods were sold abroad, the more funds came in to finance the war effort. Even things that weren't rationed quickly became hard to get, as anything that smacked of frivolity gave way to practical needs. Shoe manufacturers concentrated on soldiers' boots and sturdy shoes for the Land Girls working on the farms. Raw materials that had previously been used to make toys were redirected into more essential work, and the factories that had produced them turned to assembling radar equipment or producing guns or tanks. Few people would have denied that these were more important in the circumstances than children's tea sets and teddy bears, but it made Christmas shopping difficult.

Alcohol was another luxury that all but disappeared. Apart from the odd glass of beer, only the privileged few were able to drink during the war. But then only the privileged few had been able to afford wine and spirits before the war. For most, drinking wine was not the everyday activity it is today, and of course wine was imported. Whisky didn't have to face the U-boats, but the government would allocate the necessary cereals to distillers only if a large part of their output was exported. As one government minister put it, 'The country needs food, dollars mean food, and whisky means dollars.' In other words, what whisky there was was sold to America.

One of the reasons that most people coped as well as they did was that they were 'all in it together'. However, particularly in the cities, a black market flourished: there were always those who could get round the system. Think of Private Walker in *Dad's Army* – someone who always knew where you could get hold of cigarettes, whisky, stockings or other desirable commodities. Some took a pragmatic approach to this, grateful to be able to acquire anything that was going, at a price, and no questions asked. Others saw it as selfishness, and pretty discreditable selfishness at that. One person I spoke to while researching this book mentioned a brother who was in London during the war; he would have been in his twenties. There might have been any number of reasons why he wasn't in the forces – all sorts of 'reserved occupations' from teaching to working on the docks meant you were exempt from conscription – so I wasn't really thinking when I asked if he was in the army. 'Oh no,' his sister said. 'He wouldn't have done that. Not Jimmy.' Awkward pause from both of us. 'We weren't very proud of Jimmy.' Jimmy had obviously had ways and means of achieving his own ends – like Private Walker, deemed unfit for active service because he was allergic to corned beef. That excuse may be a comic exaggeration, but there were plenty who persuaded sympathetic doctors that they had flat feet, 'dicky' hearts or some other convenient medical condition. Clearly, more than seventy years on, Jimmy's sister was still ashamed that her brother hadn't done his bit. (He wasn't called Jimmy, by the way. Even after all this time, she didn't want me to name names.)

To revert to Christmas, although food rationing had not begun in 1939, petrol rationing had. The slogan 'Is your journey really necessary?' discouraged people from travelling even by rail. Hundreds of thousands of children had been evacuated and were spending Christmas away from their parents; and with all men aged between eighteen and forty-one obliged to register for military service (unless they were allergic to corned beef), many had been sent to France. Some shortages were already apparent and the blackout regulations that forbade the showing of any lights after dark did away with the usual bright shop-window displays and the cheerful sight of other people's Christmas trees in their front rooms. Nevertheless, the government encouraged people as far as possible to celebrate as usual, suggesting that 'reasonable expenditure on Christmas festivities will help trade and lessen unemployment'. The Women's Institute urged its members to be inventive, not to abandon its traditional parties but to 'tie its Christmas sash a little tighter'.

By 1940, attitudes had changed. Food and any form of luxury were scarcer and, with the blitz at its height, Coventry in ruins, Swansea without drinking water and other major cities constantly bombarded, there seemed little to celebrate. It was to get worse. The nightly bombing abated after Russia entered the war in 1941 and the Germans had to fight on the Eastern Front as well as the Western, but shortages remained. For Christmas 1942, the British government imported 400,000 turkeys from Ireland – which didn't go far in a country with a population of over 48 million. One shop's entire supply was designated for the Merchant Navy, while another, which normally sold six or seven thousand turkeys in the run-up to Christmas, had only six hundred, reserved by regular customers weeks in advance. By 1943, according to the diarist Vere Hodgson, not even the 'despised rabbit' was available in some shops, never mind the more highly regarded poultry. A little mutton was the best that could be hoped for. Some shops had three Christmas puddings and eight hundred registered customers.

It was against this background that the people of Britain

spent the six wartime Christmases, from 1939 to 1944. And those Christmases are what this book is about. Much of what follows consists of interviews I conducted with friends, relations, neighbours and the parents, friends, relations and neighbours of friends – people, mostly now in their eighties or nineties, who were old enough to remember what it was like. The rest is gleaned from diaries and letters written at the time, and from published books. The youngest person I spoke to was seventy-six; the oldest was nearing her hundred-and-first birthday. Their experiences were very different: urban and rural; comfortably off and achingly poor; adults longing for loved ones to come back to them; children too young to be more than vaguely aware that anything out of the ordinary was going on. There is fear, anxiety, loneliness and boredom here; but there are also frequent flashes of humour and spirit, of kindliness, community and humanity. A book like this can't hope to be comprehensive; rather it is intended as a collection of snapshots or perhaps jigsaw pieces. Gathered and assembled almost at random, they still produce – I hope – an intriguing picture of a world that was in many ways warmer, less self-centred, more stoical than ours. Even if – or perhaps because – there was a war on.

CHAPTER I

'A RUSH TO SAVE THE CHILDREN'

By the summer of 1939, it was apparent to almost everyone that the policy of appeasement had failed and that war was coming. Alongside its military plans, the government developed a strategy for keeping the nation's children safe. In the last days of August, in London and other cities, schoolchildren were instructed to bring in a case containing a change of clothes, enough food for a journey of several hours, and the gas masks that had been issued shortly before. At school, teachers fastened name tags to the children's jackets or hung labels round their necks, walked them in a crocodile to the nearest major railway station, then turned round, came back with the children and sent them home.

By no means every potential evacuee had this opportunity to rehearse. For many, the real thing – on Friday, 1 September, the day that Hitler invaded Poland – came as a bolt from the blue. Thanks to Operation Pied Piper, as it was called, toddlers were separated from their parents for the first time, while elder siblings were instructed to hold tightly to their little brother or sister's hand so that members of the same family could stay together.

Two days later, at 11.15 on the morning of Sunday the 3rd, Prime Minister Neville Chamberlain announced over the radio 'this country is at war with Germany'. By that time, hundreds of thousands of urban children – including many whose parents had privately taken or sent them away to friends or relatives – had been installed in new homes in rural areas. But 'foster' parents and the heads of schools that had taken in evacuees had no powers to keep children against their parents' wishes. Some evacuees stayed for a matter of weeks, drifting back home during the 'Phoney War' of late 1939 and early 1940, when people came to believe that the threat of bombing had been exaggerated and that the war would somehow just go away; others returned simply because parents wanted their children home or children were unbearably homesick. Still others were away for five years, seeing their parents only occasionally. For some this was the start of lifelong family friendships; for others it was a time of abject misery.

Some young evacuees even went to another continent – thousands to the United States and Canada, hundreds to Australia, New Zealand and South Africa. The King's Christmas message in 1940 referred to the breaking up of homes and families because of evacuation and to the generosity of 'the peoples of the Empire [who] have eagerly thrown open the doors of their homes to our children so that they may be spared from the strain and danger of modern war'.

> But how many more children are there here who have been moved from their homes to safer quarters?
> To all of them, at home and abroad, who are separated from their fathers and mothers, to their kind friends and hosts, and to all who love them, and to parents who will be lonely without them, from all in our dear island I wish every happiness that Christmas can bring. May the new year carry us towards victory and to happier Christmas days, when everyone will be at home together in the years to come.

It was to take a while.

In England, Jim was one of the lucky ones. At the age of twelve he was sent from south London to the village of Northiam in Sussex to stay in the home of a Mr and Mrs Skinner. Mr Skinner was the local milkman and did deliveries with a horse named Bunny pulling his cart:

> The days leading up to Christmas resulted in a hive of activity at Oak Cottage, an activity that I got fully involved in. Over the years, Mr Skinner had built up a private enterprise, selling oranges and nuts to his milk-round customers. Both the fruit and seed formed a natural contribution to the festivities. The crafty Mr Skinner had orders booked well in advance of purchasing his stock. The smell of oranges in a house, and the sight

of someone rinsing the nut fragments from their dental plate, were synonymous with the season. So with a couple of wooden crates full of oranges and sacks full of nuts it was my job to get the daily orders ready. Why oranges were always sold in sevens I will never know, nor will I know why coconuts were never included in bags of mixed nuts. When Mr Skinner loaded up his sideline on the milk cart each morning, Bunny got a little extra time to digest his tit-bits.

After my dad died in 1934, I cannot recollect too much about enjoying Christmas celebrations, but I am definitely able to call to mind the Christmas of 1939. Charles [the Skinners' eldest son] and his model-like lady came early on Christmas morning to spend the day with us. Before I tell of my fascination for his dolly bird, I must mention that they brought me a present actually wrapped in coloured paper. With excitement, I hastily opened it to find a large selection of Chinese puzzles. Those twisted metal rod things that can be difficult to separate until you discover the secret, and a better choice couldn't have been made... [There follows a rapturous description of Charles's glamorous girlfriend, who looked quite out of place in a small Sussex village.] When the five of us sat round the table for our delicious roast chicken dinner we must have represented the widest range of characters in Northiam. At teatime, when Mrs Skinner got out the cake, my memory went back a month earlier when I took the uncooked mixture, plus one penny, to the local bakers. The next day I collected it, in addition to a Sharps toffee, and took home the perfectly baked cake to Mrs Skinner.

Some evacuees' experiences were eye-opening. Frank from the East End remembers:

I was evacuated, aged seven, to rural Buckinghamshire. I say 'rural' – it was only fifty miles from London, but that was a long way for a poor kid who had never been more than about a mile from home. I don't remember much about my first Christmas – the people I was staying with had two boys of their own and I didn't feel left out, so I must have had presents, but what they were I don't recall.

What I do remember is that on Boxing Day morning, I woke up to find that it had snowed in the night. Of course it snowed in London too, but I had never seen the world turned completely white before. In Bethnal Green snow turned to grubby slush within minutes; here it was soft and clean and brilliantly white in the morning sunshine. And everything was so quiet. Normally we heard the next-door farmer's horse and cart clopping along the lane, but today everything was muffled by this soft white cushion.

That winter – 1939–40 – was one of the coldest on record, and the snow lasted for weeks. Whenever I was feeling lonely or homesick, which I did sometimes, I just looked out the window at this magical world, or went out with the other boys and made snowmen. It inevitably turned into a snowball fight, but that was something I'd never had in London either! And one morning I really thought that Santa's reindeer had paid us a visit, a bit late. My foster father laughed when he told me it was a local fox coming to see if it could raid the dustbins and leaving its delicate footprints in the snow.

John, too, eventually settled down to a happy time.

I was five when war broke out and went to Primrose Hill School in north London, but the whole school was evacuated to Maidenhead. Paddington station, platform 1, I remember it well. When we got there we were taken to what I later discovered was a school hall and then led out in groups of about ten. We went up the hill knocking on doors, looking for people who were willing to take us in. I now know that this happened all over the country, because hundreds of thousands of children were moved out of the cities in a mad rush, but for a long time it seemed extraordinary that they'd evacuated an entire infants' school without knowing where anyone was going to sleep that night.

Well, a woman did take me in but I hadn't been there more than a couple of months before I was knocked off my bike and broke my leg. I can remember being in hospital and being given an anaesthetic – a piece of gauze pressed over my face. I suppose it was chloroform. Anyway, I was in plaster from my toe to the top of my thigh and when I got out of hospital the woman I'd been staying with wouldn't have me back. So I was sent to the local children's home for a while, and then the woman's mother got to hear about it and she took me in. She had a farm about five miles out of Maidenhead, and I stayed there very happily for five years. There were three daughters in the house and two other refugees – girls from another part of London – so it was very crowded, but they were kind to me and they did make an effort at Christmas.

Being on a farm, we always had plenty of eggs and vegetables, and they kept hens, which they sold for other people's Christmas dinners: I remember us children sitting round the kitchen table plucking them. We always had chicken for Christmas dinner ourselves, but not one of our own – having kept them all year, we couldn't face eating them; they were more like pets. So we must have bought or bartered for one from someone else. Out in the country there wasn't much of a black market, but there was plenty of bartering going on.

All the cooking was done on a range, with coal, and that's how they heated the water too. Bath night was Friday, in a tin bath in front of the fire, everyone using the same water one after another. There was a small bathroom in the house, with a bathtub, but that's where we kept the coal.

No hot-water bottles, so on winter nights we heated bricks in the oven, wrapped them in newspaper and took them to bed – just as they used to in the nineteenth century. But then out in the country in the 1940s you were still pretty much in the nineteenth century.

We didn't have much in the way of presents, but I remember Christmas as a happy time. We made coloured chains from strips of sticky paper, and we cut out shapes that we hung up round the room, but it was very limited because everything was rationed. I remember a sort of soft peppermint sweet, made from flour and peppermint essence, which they must have saved from before the war – that was a real treat.

Mollie was another who was well looked after as an evacuee:

My brother and I were evacuated from London to a farm in Kent and we were very happy there. In fact, my brother – aged about ten – came home wanting to be a farmer. Back in London there seemed likely to be no meat for Christmas, so my stepmother entered a whole lot of raffles and ended up winning three chickens! They came with their feathers on and had to be plucked and drawn and their heads cut off. My stepmother, of Irish rural descent, did this without a blink, but my brother turned pale, left the room and never again mentioned a wish to be a farmer.

After the poverty of the East End, the country could seem very luxurious. Certainly it was a pleasant change not to be hungry all the time. There were other excitements, too, as Simon remembers:

We had roast goose, roast potatoes, parsnips and Brussels sprouts, followed by Christmas pudding. We weren't used to eating so much, so after the main course we all felt we needed a break. By the time we were ready for pudding, it was getting dark and we had closed the curtains. Mrs Evans went into the kitchen to collect the pudding, which had been steaming away on the range all this time. Someone put the lights out, and I'll always remember that all I could see was a strange glow coming through the doorway. It was the flame of the brandy she had poured over the pudding and set light to. I'd never seen anything so eerie. My family was Jewish, so we didn't celebrate Christmas and I'd never heard of setting fire to a pudding before. Come to think of it, it was probably the last year for many years that the Evanses had any brandy to burn.

Grace, from a big family in the East End, had expected to be lonely when billeted with just one sister in the home of an elderly, childless couple:

But they were rich beyond my wildest dreams – or so I thought when I was twelve. I'd never seen anything like their house: carpets, even in the hallway and on the stairs; sofas and armchairs with no stuffing pouring out of them; warm beds and a proper bathroom. At home, we'd had to go outside to the privy, which we shared with three other families. My sister and I woke up on Christmas morning expecting it to be like any other day, only to find little pillowcases full of presents at the foot of our beds. Not only an apple and some nuts, but bright pink hair ribbons, pink hair grips in the shape of butterflies, and cotton handkerchiefs with our initials embroidered on them. Auntie Win, as we called our foster mother, had obviously been to a lot of trouble to make Christmas special for us – and even these little gifts were incredibly luxurious to girls who'd never had anything pretty before.

Audrey, too, had three very happy years as an evacuee:

I was privately evacuated, when I was nine, to my aunt and uncle in Dorset. At home in south London we shared air-raid shelters with our neighbours; I was in one and my parents were in another when a bomb dropped very close up and a fireman had to dig me out. After that, my mother thought I would be safer in the country.

My aunt and uncle had no children of their own and they treated me just like their own daughter and made sure I had a lovely Christmas, even though I was away from my parents. The thing I remember most clearly is my uncle going out into the garden and bringing in a huge tree and decorating it. He planted it in the garden every January and brought it indoors for a few weeks every December, but it must have been around for a good few years, because it was enormous.

Kay from Glasgow had a lucky escape, but still not a very happy time:

Glasgow was very heavily bombed, with air raids night after night, and it was arranged that my sisters and I would be evacuated to an uncle in Canada. For some reason my father cancelled the arrangement just two days before the ship was due to sail – and that ship was torpedoed in the Atlantic, killing seventy-seven children.

But my parents still thought we would be safer away from Glasgow, so my older sister and I were sent to Lockerbie, where we stayed for a year in the home of the town clerk's wife. She wasn't cruel to us, but she didn't really want us. I can't blame her – she had two sons of her own – but she didn't treat us as part of the family. I remember that we had to do our own washing and I still have the mark of where I got my hand caught in the wringer. And we had our meals – including our Christmas dinner – downstairs with the maids.

I remember being very jealous of our younger sister, who got to stay home with Mum; the few times she came to visit she seemed to be dressed in pretty things, and by comparison I thought we were in rags. But the worst thing was hearing that there had been air raids at home and not knowing what had happened to our parents. We literally wouldn't know if they were alive or dead. It was very distressing for two small girls, aged about seven and nine.

For Millie, too, being in the country was a mixed blessing:

> Life in the farmhouse centred round the kitchen – the one room that was always warm. My bedroom was so cold in the winter that before I went to bed I used to lay out my clothes for the morning in the order that I would put them on: underwear, then blouse and skirt, then jumper, so that there was no frantic searching for clean knickers as I stood shivering in my pyjamas. The sooner I was dressed, the sooner I could get downstairs to the warmth of the kitchen range.
>
> There was a room that my 'auntie', as I called her, referred to as 'the parlour', but it was kept for best and we children weren't normally allowed in. There was a proper fireplace, but we only had a fire there on special occasions. The only time I remember going in there was on Christmas Eve, when the vicar came round for a glass of sherry and we all had to sit quietly while the grown-ups talked. It was much more comfortable to be released back to the kitchen, where the Christmas tree was and where we were allowed to sit on the floor and play.

Arthur was miserable as an evacuee:

> I've never been as lonely as I was that first Christmas away from home. I wasn't used to a big family – the people I was billeted with had four children, all older than me, and on Christmas Day some neighbours or cousins or something came round, too. It felt as if there

were about twenty people in that little house – and at home, there were just my mum and dad and me. While we were waiting for dinner to be ready I went and sat at the bottom of the garden, and looked at the hens. It was freezing, but it was better than sitting indoors listening to all those people talking at once and knowing that I didn't belong.

My present from my parents was a jigsaw puzzle. It was one of the 'Victory' series and showed an Imperial Airways Empire Flying Boat, 'dissected', so that you could see what was going on inside. I sat on the floor and did it over and over again that Christmas, thinking about my parents and hoping that they were thinking of me. I don't know what happened to that jigsaw, but at the end of the war Victory brought out a 'Spitfires in Flight' puzzle and I have that in my attic to this day.

Others had far worse experiences than loneliness. A book of evacuees' memories published in the eighties contained a contribution from a man who, having written at length about his foster mother's cruelty at other times of the year, recorded what happened one Christmas:

On Christmas Day I had a clockwork tanker truck given to me. She let me wind up the lorry and as I removed the key she took the key and allowed the toy to run down. She refused to give me back the key. Remembering that I had lost keys to toys before and pushed cars backwards and released them, I did the same with the toy truck. It worked perfectly.

At this she called me a 'Damn young shit!' and hit me over the head with a chair. (I have the scar today.) By now it was 11 a.m., so she told me to fetch wood and stay out.

It was after dark when I was allowed back in the house. I was hurting with a large bump on my head and freezing with the cold. She then made me wash in cold water. Her daughter was given the lorry.

He was eight years old.

Brian, born in Surrey, was sent to Cornwall when his parents became worried about the bombing.

I was five when war broke out, so I do have some memories before then: I remember the taste of bananas and ice cream, two things we didn't see all the way through the war. Even once the war was over, if word got around that there was a shop or a van selling ice cream, you'd dash over there to find there was a queue half a mile long.

What triggered my parents' sending me away was a bomb falling nearby. I was sleeping downstairs, in my parents' bed, and the ceiling fell in. I'm told that I woke up and said, 'Was that a bomb, Daddy?' Dad said, 'Yes, go back to sleep', and I did. But in the morning I couldn't get out of bed – the bedclothes were covered in plaster dust and were too heavy for me to move.

So my parents sent me to a farm where we had been a couple of times on holiday, just outside Bude in Cornwall. I remember being lonely and homesick; I wrote grizzling letters asking to be allowed to come home, but the farmer's wife must have censored them and assured my parents I was having a good time. I didn't see them for two years.

Nowadays, those memories come back to me almost as if in sepia, like pictures from Elizabethan England. I remember most of my time on the farm vividly. I experienced no cruelty. I was treated almost exactly the same way as the couple's own children (two boys – one a year older than me, one two years younger – and a girl older than all of us). Inexplicably, I never went to school. Instead I simply played around or worked on the farm, collecting hens' eggs every morning, hand-milking the cows, ploughing with a heavy horse, picking potatoes until my back nearly broke, helping with the harvest, etc. But the farmers were dirt poor. Although I collected the eggs every day, I don't think I ate one all the time I was there. They all had to be sold.

What I remember most of all is being hungry all the time: I pulled up carrots from the garden or went foraging for blackberries and nuts to get more to eat. I remember Kellogg's Puffed Wheat for breakfast, and for dinner rabbit stew featured large, with carrots and onions. I was the one who set traps for the rabbits, and I learned to gut them and even to whack them on the head to finish them off: quite an experience for a suburban lad who can't have been more than eight.

Miraculously I suffered nothing worse than malnutrition and, on looking back, I feel the experience actually enriched my life.

Although I have these clear memories, for some reason I have no recollection of Christmas on the farm. Maybe everyone was too poor even to celebrate it, although we went to church in Poughill every Sunday, travelling there and back by horse and cart, so I assume we went on Christmas Day too. It was on one of these journeys to church, in December, that I fell out of the cart and broke my arm.

I remember looking at my arm and seeing that my sleeve and the arm inside it were bent. It didn't hurt at all at the time – though it certainly did later. I was taken to the local cottage hospital, where they couldn't cope with me and sent me to Exeter. There, the first thing they did was stand me up in a bathtub and, of all things, give me an enema. Then I had a bath and they scrubbed me very thoroughly. I must have been very ragged and dirty; they were cleaning me inside and out before putting me in their nice white sheets. Then they proceeded to feed me up wonderfully – or so it seemed to me. Whether there were extra rations because it was Christmas, I don't know, but it was the first time for two years that I hadn't been hungry.

Brian was sent home after the accident, and he wasn't the only one. Keith, aged eight, was evacuated from Liverpool to North Wales, where he lived for a few weeks with a professor, his wife and two sons, in a house that was much more luxurious than his own, overlooking the Menai Strait:

it had a garden that seemed huge to me and there was a tree house. I had never seen one before and I loved it and was terrified of it at the same time. The professor's sons were a couple of years older than me and sometimes they would let me play in it and sometimes they wouldn't.

One day we'd been sent outside to play because the professor's wife was baking. I think she was making the Christmas cake; it was certainly a bitterly cold day, so it was quite late in the year. Anyway, we three boys were all in the tree house together and they suddenly seemed to change their minds about letting me join in. I could always tell when they were going to be mean to me, because they would start speaking Welsh, knowing that I didn't understand. Anyway, somehow or other I fell out of the tree house and broke my leg. I had some time in hospital but was sent home for Christmas and stayed there, so I spent the war in Liverpool after all. We weren't near the docks, so we were never actually bombed and I remember being more excited than scared at all the planes going overhead. I think I felt safer at home than I did in that tree house – and I'll never know if the professor's sons pushed me out.

Not all evacuation was carried out through Operation Pied Piper. Some parents simply chose to send or take their children away, in order to keep them safe. Brenda remembers:

That period of my life is a bit hazy to me. I was seven years old and, although war hadn't been declared, my sister, brother [aged twelve and nine] and I were evacuated a week before 3 September 1939, away from the imminent bombing of London. It wasn't official: Mum took us to her birthplace in Aberdeen, because she didn't want us all to be separated and sent to different parts of the country. That might have happened, because we were at different schools, and whole schools were evacuated together.

The four of us moved in with my grandmother and my two unmarried aunts, Mum's sisters, while my father stayed working in London. My mother did all the cooking for the household, as both my aunts went out to work. She also did all the shopping and took our ration books with her. At that time I was the only one in the household who had a green ration book [issued to pregnant women, nursing mothers and small children], which entitled me to purchase bananas, when they were in the shops – which was hardly ever. I don't think we had a banana until after the war.

Mum worked very hard looking after us all and I remember one Christmas my big sister and I decided to bake a cake for her as a treat. Mum was out at the shops – queuing up for something, no doubt. We were so proud at how the cake turned out. When she came home and saw it, she was absolutely livid, as we had used up the whole of our ration of sugar for the week.

We didn't do much that was special at Christmas: this being Scotland, Hogmanay was the chosen time for celebration. We even had chicken on that day (our once-a-year treat). I do remember making chains out of crepe paper, which I expect my brother then strung up for me; and the stockings on the mantelpiece which awaited the three of us and which contained an orange, an apple and some nuts.

We must have had other presents, though, because I remember vividly there was a strict rule about opening them: we weren't allowed to start until the adults were ready. On Christmas morning we were all in the living room except my auntie Minnie, who was great fun and always joking about something. We heard a clip-clopping noise from outside, and someone ringing a bell, mimicking the sound of departing reindeer. A moment later Auntie Minnie came in, looked out the window and said, 'Father Christmas has gone now.' Then we were allowed to open our presents.

Kathleen was four and living in Portsmouth, an important port, when war broke out. Shortly after her sixth birthday one of her much older brothers was killed in the Battle of Crete, a tragedy her parents didn't mention to her until the war was over four years later. Portsmouth was a frequent target of bombing raids, so Kathleen's mother arranged for her to be evacuated to the village of Swanmore, about fifteen miles away:

It wasn't a normal life, as my mother billeted me with a really lovely family while she came and went to Portsmouth: she still had her husband and one surviving son living in a shattered city, bombed day and night. She stayed with me in our rented room from Monday to Friday as I was at school in Swanmore, but she left me in the care of the landlady Mrs Goff for the weekend. She did this for obvious reasons, I know now: if our small home in Portsmouth had been bombed, then at least one of the family would have lived on in peace in the Hampshire countryside.

Christmases came and went very frugally. There were no kitchen facilities in our one attic room – Mum cooked on an oil cooker – but those yellow powdered eggs I do remember, and fresh milk straight from the farm down the road. The best meal came from getting our wellington boots on and going out early in the morning for a bucket of mushrooms. Other than that, the clearest Christmas memory I have is looking out the window and seeing my next-door neighbour George riding his new bicycle down the road – it must have been a Christmas present and I just longed for one for myself.

Many years later, I moved to New Zealand, where I have lived ever since – and where Christmas is very different, with drinks on the lawn in the middle of summer, followed by a traditional turkey dinner later in the day when it's cool enough for people to want to eat it. At one time I attended a creative-writing class, run by a very accomplished lady who reminded me of Joyce Grenfell. She set us a lot of homework about wartime, with titles like 'What a Rotten Gift' and 'Not Sausages Again!' I particularly remember this poem I wrote – most of it genuine childhood memories, with a bit of poetic licence. It shows that we did manage to make Christmas special, despite everything.

A Child's Memories of Christmas

Jingle Bells, mistletoe
Wading through the soft white snow
Faces wrapped in warm bright scarves
Coming home to a fireside glow.

Joining friends for carol singing
Gentle knocks on a stranger's door
'Away in a Manger' – 'Silent Night' –
Isn't it nice when they ask for more?

Pretending to sleep with one eye open
Watching the bedroom door
Will Santa in his long red robes
Leave my presents on the bedroom floor?

Christmas Day has dawned at last
There are presents at the end of the bed
A dolly, some books, a painting set
A dressing gown and slippers in matching red.

I can smell breakfast cooking so I'd better go down
Poor Mother's been baking all week
My brothers have built a huge snowman in the garden
Through my curtains I've had a quick peek.

This is the day we have friends round for dinner
A day most unlike any other
I wonder will Dad put a sixpence in the pudding
Especially for me to discover.

I've waited all year for this wonderful day,
The day we feel love for each other
But my brothers will chase me and tease me
And I'll run off and hide behind Mother.

One piece of poetic licence: I didn't get all those presents – they're there to make up the rhythm and the rhyme. I did get one dolly, though, which I named Vera, as the wireless had Vera Lynn singing all the time. I kept that doll for twenty years, but left her in the wardrobe when I moved to New Zealand. I have often regretted leaving Vera behind.

Betty, an older neighbour of Kathleen's, was evacuated from Portsmouth with her school. They moved to Salisbury in September 1939, and in November Betty's mother wrote to the headmistress asking permission for her daughter to come home for Christmas. Although the bombing of Portsmouth hadn't yet started, the headmistress was taking no risks and wrote a firm letter saying, 'You must accept full responsibility for having her home. You would need to send me a written statement to that effect with the exact dates.' Betty stayed at school, where a letter from the Lord Mayor of Portsmouth, addressed to all evacuated children, wishing them well and hoping that they were grateful to those who had looked after them, would have given little comfort.

Keeping the family together was, understandably, a priority for many parents. Ronnie's mother held out against evacuation as long as she could:

I was born in the East End of London, in Bromley-by-Bow, and wasn't quite three when war broke out. Most of the local kids were evacuated, but my mum wouldn't let us go – my dad was in the Merchant Navy and away all the time, so I guess she wanted to keep the rest of the family together as best she could.

Then when I was five we were down in the air-raid shelter when the block of flats we lived in was bombed. It was completely destroyed and left us with only the clothes we stood up in. And we hadn't had much to start with – we don't have many photos of that time, but there is one of me in a jumper so big it has had to be pinned together to stay on me. It's obviously handed down from someone much older who had grown out of it.

After the bombing we were sent to Rickmansworth in Hertfordshire, which was practically the countryside then – Rickmansworth was no more than a village. We stayed in a big house with a number of other families, and to us kids it was paradise, being outside all the time, scrumping for apples and looking for snakes – Rickmansworth was full of adders in those days. The people there were kind to us, but they didn't let us mix with their own children. We were probably a bit too rough and scruffy for them.

My first Christmas there was the first time I tasted chocolate and I remember I didn't like it. I just wasn't used to such rich food. Our Christmas treat was always chicken: Mum belonged to some sort of club where you put a bit of money away each week, so you could afford a chicken at Christmas. Then the bones and remains went into a stew for the next day – nothing was wasted.

We used to really look forward to Christmas. We used to chop up firewood and sell it to make a bit of money to buy presents, but we made a lot of things too: some of the older boys even made their own cricket bats. I remember being given comics like *The Dandy* and *The Beano*, and once my brother got a box of lead soldiers; nothing fancy, but these things were really treasured. People came round with a tin bath full of toys: they must have had some sort of whip-round for the evacuees, so everyone was given something. We didn't have a tree, but I do remember making paper chains, and because we were in the country there was mistletoe.

One time my dad must have had leave, because he came home with a parrot as a present for us. We thought this was wonderful, but Mum soon discovered that, having spent some years living with sailors, the parrot's language was so bad that we had to get rid of it. She was quite strict, my mum, and brought us up to be polite, so she didn't want the parrot to be a bad influence!

After we'd moved back to London, towards the end of the war, I remember Christmases in a big hall in Hackney, with everyone getting together for a knees-up. My brother would stand in the middle of the room, using a walking stick as a conductor's baton, and we'd sing all the old Cockney songs, 'My Old Man Said Follow the Van', 'Knees Up, Mother Brown' and that sort of thing. Everyone would chip in a few pence, so there was a small barrel of beer.

I always remember a happy Christmas. In fact, I remember nothing but a happy childhood. We had nothing, but everyone looked after everyone else – if anyone suffered a bereavement or had a problem, people would rally round. I think it's because we were all in the same boat – there was no competition between people. People talk about being born with a silver spoon, but that's all rubbish. It's what you make of yourself.

David had two quite different experiences as an evacuee, four years apart. He was living in Beckenham, Kent, where there was no official evacuation. But when they were bombed out in 1940, he, his mother, elder brother and younger sister went to Kingsteignton in Devon, just outside Newton Abbot. David was ten:

We stayed with a Mr Glanfield, who had been a driver with the Canadian Pacific Railroad in its pioneering days. His house was part of a terrace and the gardens at the back were 'in common' – long strips with no fences between them and all the sheds against one wall. Mr Glanfield's shed was made of railway sleepers, tarred black, and we used to play in there: it was full of his old brown tin trunks, with bits and pieces from his travels, and tin hatboxes that had belonged to his wife. He had a collection of *Boy's Own* comics dating back to the 1870s and it was marvellous for me to be able to read them and imagine what his boyhood must have been like. The garden also backed on to the local bakery, so that part of the wall was quite warm. I remember the window was kept locked, but we use to make signs to the men working inside that we'd like a cake. We never got one, though.

Mother had taken us children to Devon with a few suitcases, but at Christmas Dad came down with a large trunk to augment what she'd been able to carry – he brought extra bed-clothing and things like that. Inevitably his train was delayed; he arrived at Newton Abbot at something like three in the morning. Of course there were no buses or anything and he started to walk the mile or so to Kingsteignton. Mr Coppin, the postman, had been collecting mail in Newton Abbot and was cycling to the village, passing the racecourse that is there to this day, when he overtook my dad, struggling with this heavy trunk. Between them they manoeuvred it on to his bicycle frame and pushed it to Fore Street, where we were staying. Dad must have known that Mr Glanfield slept downstairs and didn't want to wake him, so he threw stones at my mother's window upstairs. She came down, let him in and so Christmas began.

Dad also had our presents in that trunk. I remember I'd requested a Spitfire – a balsa wood model – but I was given a Defiant instead. The Defiant was an earlier fighter plane, designed to carry two people, with the gunner sitting behind the pilot; I've read about them since and know that they were very useful aircraft. But to a boy of ten, for whom the Spitfire was a sort of golden chalice, it was very disappointing. I've a horrible feeling I showed that I was disappointed, which is a great shame considering the trouble my dad had gone to.

My brother and I were also given stamp albums: I remember them very clearly and I remember that we were able to build up our collections thanks to all the elderly widows who were living in Kingsteignton at the time. These were women whose husbands had fought in the First World War and even the Boer War, and either had been killed there or had died in the intervening years. There were no air-raid shelters in the village, so when a siren went off we scattered to the various larger houses and took shelter there. I used to talk about stamps to these ladies, several of whom then produced letters they'd received from their husbands in South Africa, still in their envelopes, and let me have the Victorian stamps.

The Glanfields were Methodists and they had an organ in the house. My mother was a trained pianist, so she used to play the organ, but she wasn't used to pumping the foot pedals – I would lie on the floor and pump them for her. Mr Glanfield would get out his violin and I have clear memories of us all singing carols and hymns, and old songs like 'Drink to Me Only With Thine Eyes', to the accompaniment of organ and violin.

As for food, Dad was a butcher's manager and even during the war he was able to bring us a turkey – we didn't go short. I was often sent to the local market garden, about a mile away, to collect vegetables, and there was a farm nearby where they didn't seem to know there was a war on. I was friendly with Ronnie, the farmer's son, and would help him out when he was helping his dad. His mum used to reward us with clotted cream sandwiches – thick, thick cream, which they shouldn't have been making. It meant they were skimming the cream off the milk before they sold it, which was against the law.

We'd very occasionally get an orange, but that was a real Christmas treat. Dad had friends in the RAF who were based in Gibraltar and they used to bring them back: I expect he swapped them for a few sausages.

David and his family moved back to Beckenham in 1941, when the threat of bombing reduced. But in 1944 the doodlebug attacks began and they were evacuated again, this time officially and to a village outside Nottingham. By now, David's brother had left school and was working, so there was only himself, his mother and his sister.

A lot of people in the villages outside Nottingham where what I would call nouveaux riches: they had grown rich from producing munitions, but they seemed to be quite selfish. The billeting officer who was trying to find homes for us all got very fed up with excuses such as 'We have illness in the house' as a reason for not taking in evacuees. But eventually he found us a little eighteenth-century farmer's cottage, quite near where the 'lord of the manor' lived. In sharp contrast to the other rich people around, he and his wife were very kind to us. The lady offered my mother vegetables from her lovely walled garden and let me go and dig them up whenever I liked.

The cottage had electricity but no gas, so the cooking was done on an old-fashioned range – and it was much more efficient than the electric oven we had at home. That Christmas lunch was the best I had ever tasted.

The winter of 1944–5 was harsh. The fields flooded and then froze over. I had made friends with a girl in the village who had a sledge and we had a wonderful time pulling each other across the ice. I also remember the hoar frost thick on the fields and the hedges when we walked Dad and my brother back to the outskirts of Nottingham after their brief Christmas visit. We crossed the Halfpenny Bridge (you had to pay a halfpenny to cross it) to where they could get a tram to take them to the station and it was bitterly cold. But very beautiful.

There was one unpleasant incident that Christmas, though. The cottage was basically 'one up, one down', so my mother, sister and I were all sleeping in the same room and I had gone to bed first. There was a lovely little brown mouse – a field mouse, I guess – playing around the fireplace in the bedroom, and I was delighted to be watching it. Then my mother and sister came up and they screamed and insisted I do something about it. Very reluctantly, I bashed the mouse with my shoe and threw it out the window into the snow. Next morning my mother assured me that it had gone – it must have scampered off, she said, so I hadn't killed it and I wasn't to worry. But I was sure that a cat or an owl had got it and have always regretted hurting that lovely mouse.

It wasn't only the children who had to deal with changes, of course: things were strange for their host families too. Elsie was a young mother living in a Gloucestershire village. With two daughters of her own and a husband fighting in North Africa, she took in two evacuees and did her best to 'make a Christmas' for them:

With four children in the house, aged between six and ten, I really wanted to do something special. We grew our own vegetables, but almost everything else was in short supply – including dried fruit for the Christmas pudding. Like lots of people, I bumped up the mixture with turnip and beetroot from the garden. I don't think it did much for the taste, but at least the beetroot improved the colour.

As for presents, we had a sort of 'bring and buy' in the church hall and one of my neighbours, whose children had grown up, brought all sorts of games and toys. I was able to give the girls Ludo, snakes and ladders, and dominoes, which we all played together on Christmas afternoon. And I gave the little boy a spinning top. His family wasn't well off and he had never seen such a thing. By the end of Boxing Day I was regretting it, because it had bashed against me and the furniture I don't know how many times, but I'd never seen the lad so happy.

Irvine remembers a poignant tale of evacuees in the north:

It was 1940 and Christmas was coming. I was ten years old and lived with my grandparents in Blackpool. Down in the south, London was being heavily bombed by the Germans, and suddenly trainloads of evacuees were pouring into Blackpool in an attempt to escape the destruction.

My granddad and I were bringing home a Christmas tree and were surprised when we reached our road to find it was overflowing with children. A crocodile of evacuees was snaking along the pavement and spilling over onto the tarmac. Each child carried a bag or a small suitcase of belongings. They all wore labels, tied onto their clothes, bearing their name and age. None of them had their parents with them. They were all part of a frightening rush to save the children.

In the street there were a dozen helpers, and I saw my teacher among them. As the children waited on the pavement, the helpers began knocking desperately at door after door. People came out to see what was happening and the helpers begged them to take in a child, to give them a home. Sometimes curtains fluttered and doors remained closed, but little by little the children were taken into their new homes and the queue moved further up the road.

Nan and Granddad took in two sisters, Elsie and Margaret. Elsie was seven and Margaret nine. They were very different from us. They looked poor and underfed, and they were cold; their cotton dresses were too thin for our northern weather. We found out that they had never been on a train before and that they and many of the other children had wept, wrenched from home.

Nan, who had been a midwife, soon made the girls welcome and we all had a meal together. She showed them their room, which had pretty curtains. As we had only one hot-water bottle, Granddad went out and bought another, and the girls got one each, hugging them tightly when bedtime came. For the first time they laughed. They told us they had never had a hot-water bottle before.

Then the girls' mother came to see them, bringing them their Christmas present. She was small, with dark hair, thin like her children and white-faced. It was a joyful reunion. The girls told their mum how they had hot-water bottles, and that the curtains were all flowers. Nan and Granddad were told how the home next door had been hit with an incendiary bomb, but theirs had escaped. And how there was a chance they would be found a new place to live on London's outskirts so they could all be together again.

The visit was all too short and the mother left by an afternoon train.

I wrote that she had brought the girls their Christmas present. I was shocked when I saw what it was. Each girl was given a comic. At first I couldn't believe that that was all they were going to get. Each comic was rolled up neatly and tied with a piece of tinsel. I glanced at the heap of parcels that waited at the foot of our Christmas tree and felt a wave of shame. It seemed that I was to receive so much and they so little.

The girls were delighted with their presents. They kept them tied up, and placed them unopened at the foot of the tree to await opening on Christmas morning. And quietly other gifts for the girls were added.

But the comics… and their mother. Over the years I have realised that love and the comics were all the poor woman had.

CHAPTER 2

'THANK GOODNESS...
NOW WE CAN GET
SOME SLEEP'

Life in a wartime city was appreciably more dangerous than life in the country. Although bombs could fall anywhere if a pilot got lost or had 'spares' to unload, the targets for raids were generally major ports and industrial centres – not only London, but Birmingham, Glasgow, Liverpool, Manchester, Portsmouth, Plymouth and many more. Percentage-wise, the most severely damaged city of all was Hull, with half its population made homeless and 95 per cent of houses damaged; many people left town at night to sleep in the fields. In 1942, the 'Baedeker raids', named after the popular German series of travel guides, also attacked such cities as Exeter, Bath, Norwich and York. (But, bizarrely, not Oxford. Hitler apparently liked Oxford and intended to base himself there after the planned invasion, so he didn't want it damaged.) These places were of cultural rather than military significance, and the strategy was to have the greatest possible effect on civilian life and on national morale. The V-1s and V-2s – the 'doodlebugs' and rockets of 1944 and 1945, the vast majority of which fell on or near London – also aimed at maximum disruption. The combined effect was that, in the course of six years, some 67,000 British civilians were killed and perhaps double that number injured, mostly in urban areas.

In anticipation of war, between February and September 1939 the government produced one and a half million galvanised steel shelters, built from a number of straight (for the sides) and curved (for the roof) panels. They came to be known as Anderson shelters, after the then Lord Privy Seal Sir John Anderson, who had special responsibility for preparing the country to protect itself against air raids. Anderson shelters were issued free to those who earned less than five pounds a week – and that was a lot of people, with the average factory worker's wage being about four pounds – and cost seven pounds for those earning more. Dug into back gardens, half-buried and covered with a layer of soil, Andersons were designed to accommodate up to six people and were often shared between neighbours. Shelters were also built in school grounds and other places where large numbers were at risk. Some Andersons were fitted with a drainage sump, but there was no built-in floor, so they tended to be cold and damp. Many people furnished them with mattresses, blankets, torches and other basics and during the worst of the bombing raids slept there every night. The most nervous – or the most pragmatic – simply went down into the shelter and stayed there; others waited for the siren warning of a raid to sound, then came back indoors once the 'all clear' signal was given.

Also supplied free to those on low incomes was the indoor Morrison shelter, named after Herbert Morrison, the Minister for Home Security. Two feet six inches (75 centimetres) high and about the size of a small double bed, it consisted of a mattress base, wire-meshed sides and a heavy steel table-style top.

Those without access to a purpose-built shelter took refuge in pre-existing structures, most famously the London Underground stations; under railway arches; in the basements of large buildings; in their own cellars; in a cupboard under the stairs; or simply under a sturdy table. When the raid was over, they came out and got on with their lives. One woman living not far from Glasgow remembers, as a small child, hearing planes overhead; her mother told her that they were bombers and calmly carried on writing her Christmas cards.

One of the best accounts we have of 'how unimportant people in London and Birmingham lived through the war years' comes from the diaries of Vere Hodgson. Originally from Birmingham, and with a mother and sister still there, Vere lived in the Notting Hill area of London throughout the war, doing welfare work at a place known as the Sanctuary, under the auspices of a Miss Moyes. Like Rose's letters later in the book, her memories of Christmas demonstrate how life became harder and shortages worse at the years passed. To begin, in December 1940:

Saturday, 21st

Have sent off lots of parcels of clothes; and we are giving toys to all the children in the Public Shelter opposite our Shelter in China Walk, Lambeth, Miss M. is giving the people a hot supper on Xmas Eve…hot pies and mince pies. Then in our own Shelter the women will have a good dinner on Christmas Day. From here we have given many women 10/- [ten shillings – 50p] *to help them, also clothes and toys if there were children. It was so nice finding things to fit them.*

Sunday, 22nd

Slept well, but work very cold in the early hours and expected snow. Came down to Sanctuary. Heard that a bomber had come down on Victoria Station the previous night at 7 p.m. That was the queer wonk I heard. It descended with all its bombs on Ebury Bridge. The Station is unusable today, and everyone had to go by bus to Clapham Junction to pick up trains. Guns are working away outside. Observer [newspaper] *is very emphatic for us to watch for invasion this Christmas. I don't know about getting down to Brum…there are no extra trains and I fear they will be full.*

A year later, both shopping and travel were tougher:

Friday, 19th

Managed to get a pound of apples out of the Old Pole [the local greengrocer]. *Also some prunes. He is quite kind to*

*me. Burning question is…shall we who are braving the Ban
on Travel get home for Christmas! News from stations is
conflicting. Some say all people are getting on – others that
hundreds are left behind. I feel my journey on Tuesday will
not be without adventure.*

Sunday, 28th

*A journey almost without adventure!… I managed to leave
the office at 4.30 p.m. Miss Moyes departed early – so
dark had been the picture painted concerning the fate of
travellers over Xmas. We just hoped that everyone else would
be frightened – and leave the trains for us. Barishnikov* [a
Russian colleague] *amused himself with tales of broken ribs
and barricaded platforms* […]

*The truth was far otherwise. Paddington at 5 p.m.
resembled a deserted village platform – a few folk wandering
about – a mild queue here and there. I consulted a porter.
He told me confidentially that if I wanted to avoid the crush
I should proceed to the end of this platform, and approach
No. 2 from the other side. I thanked him, and padded
along. Crossed the bridge, and was faced with a stern
portress who demanded my ticket, and seemed amazed I
wanted to go on so early.*

*The Cardiff train, they said, had to load and depart
before train from Brum could come in. I watched the
travellers. In came Cardiff and one for Swansea. People all
snug and warm were settled, when an important person
strode on to the platform and seeing the Swansea train with
only about one person in every compartment, gave orders*

that only one train was to run! So all the Cardiff people were tipped out into the one for Swansea.

Still there seemed no particular crowds streaming in for the Birmingham train. We were just a thin line. In short, I have never travelled so comfortably! Had a corner seat. There was a nice little girl and her Mother who got out at Banbury. Snow Hill is all mended from the bomb and looks tidy.

In 1942, even such basics as apples and onions had become rare and expensive:

Sunday, 13th

Thought I was going to be clever and get some Chinese figs for Xmas. Waiting in shop for ten minutes only to be told: A sweet ration and a half! Ruefully left the shop. Don't know what they will manage to get at home. As long as we have Bread Sauce with an onion, I don't mind.

By Christmas 1944, food was easier ('We all managed to get a plum pudding'), but travel more difficult:

I was warned that on Paddington station at 4 p.m. they were queuing for the 6.10 p.m. to Birmingham [...] We were obliged to circle the streets outside, streams of us, but eventually we reached the main line station. Here throngs were moving in all directions at once, with luggage. I eventually found my queue – twenty abreast and one hundred deep! Was I right – yes, a likely looking man informed me, for the 6.10. I waited for one hour and forty minutes. Packed solid. People seemed to be standing on my feet, or resting their luggage on them. I could dimly feel my own stuff, but had lost hold of the handle, and feared someone would mizzle my Xmas Pudding […]

At 6.20 p.m. there was a move. Everyone bent down with renewed exhilaration to seize their luggage – and with a mad rush we swept on to the platform. The train for Birmingham was in!

Of course, by the time I got there it was full…I struggled on down. My rubber boots seemed to slither all over the place. I felt I could do no more… But I put my head despairingly in a carriage… 'Is there one seat?' Yes… was the welcome reply, and a soldier lifted my case and basket. I sank down exhausted. The bliss of the moment. I had got in.

Viola was also living in London and keeping a diary. During the autumn of 1940 she had slept in the cellar almost every night and faced Christmas with mixed emotions:

Monday Dec 16th

Went shopping today and the sweet shops are a pathetic sight. Everything in the windows is dummy, & quite a small choice inside, though Barretts had a lot of nice expensive sweets. Can't get toffees at all. Wish I'd bought things earlier, but how could I know! Even the mixed sweets are dummies.

A few days later, staying with friends in Sutton, Surrey:

Friday Dec 20th

A nice tea — they mix butter and margarine together and have it in neat pats, and as neither of them take sugar there was no shortage of that. Then we sat in the other room till supper, before 8 p.m.... Back to the drawing room, looking at cards, chatting, knitting, and at 9 came into the dining room and played Lexicon, a card game of spelling words, till past 11. Oh, how glad I was to go to bed, my face all hot & strained with talking & listening.

Gas stove alight in bedroom, hot water bottle, wash basin with hot & cold water, standard light on table by bed — a real bed at last, with soft sheets.

Christmas Eve

I've trailed ivy and glitter down the sides of the cellar stairs, & pinned up some very old Xmas cards sent me when a baby. How queer it all seems! No warning yet, 7.15 p.m., so I'm alone down here...

I've decorated the little tree, but shall have to grope for it in the dark tomorrow as breakfast will be before light — I don't remember recording before that 'Summertime' is remaining throughout winter, so it's now only dim light at 8.30 a.m.; but on the other hand, by having tea at 4.30 we always have it in daylight.

Christmas Day

A quiet night & day. Ivan decorated the cellar as well as the hall, & there are fairy lights down here. I got up at 6.45 a.m., the queerest Christmas morning, but happy, & we had our gifts at breakfast, & then went into the breakfast room to receive his to us. We walked to church down Brighton Road, but walked back via Langley Park, & Sylvia conducted the tour by pointing out where bombs had fallen, & we stopped & looked at a demolished house with only the staircase left above the ground floor. A depressing walk home! [...]

It did seem strange when we walked to Church yesterday to see Sylvia, Hilda, Ivan and J. A. all with their gas masks slung on their backs. I looked out for others & saw none at all. I wonder if they were the only ones who took them? When I told Hilda she said the Government asked everyone to carry them, & she felt it only right to do as they asked.

Monday Dec 30th

Bad raid on London last night, sky aglow. We learnt it was the City. Guildhall is gutted, a Wren church badly damaged. Firemen were playing their hoses on St Paul's all the time to save it from fire.

I was speaking to Eric Coard yesterday; we agreed Christmas might have been much worse & had been rather wonderful. Then he added that everything all through had been wonderful, that Germany had the power to smash us & yet we'd come through, & then I added my bit, that in all our own experiences too, things had been wonderful,

43

right from the beginning. It's amazing & heartening to think back & realise what we've been brought through.

Today I went shopping & tried to get Velveeta [a sort of processed cheese]. *Tried Stevenson & Rush, International Hudsons, Home Garden, Kinghams, no luck. Then at lower Sainsbury's saw a pile of round cheese boxes labelled 'for regular customers only' & further on a pile not labelled, & at last after all these months got one. There were only about eight in the pile & I don't suppose they'd have let me have two.*

Another marvel has been our Xmas dinner. Turkeys were prohibited, so Sylvia chose as large a fowl as she could, and had to pay £1 for it, & said even then it would only do for two dinners as we were nine on Christmas Day. She was upset when Sainsbury's sent two small ones & said she didn't know how we were going to make do.

Everyone had plenty on both holidays and the cold chicken lasted for three *more dinners, Friday, Saturday & Monday and then nice soup. I doubt if the usual 30/-* [thirty shillings – £1.50] *turkey would have done more than that! Elaine cooked them beautifully, also stuffing & bread sauce, it was the nicest Christmas dinner I can ever remember!*

What Viola called a 'bad raid on London' was what became known as the Second Great Fire of London. London had been bombed on fifty-six out of fifty-seven nights from 7 September 1940 onwards. This 'blitz' continued through October and November, then December brought a brief lull.

Roy, aged ten and living in Ealing, west London, remembers Christmas Eve:

For night after night after night the sirens had always sounded, any time from about four o'clock onwards. If they didn't sound, people used to say, 'They're a bit late tonight, aren't they? It's twenty past six.' The evening raids would be rather intermittent, but by nine o'clock the pattern was familiar, the constant drone. If they were late, people were unsettled; then the air-raid siren would go and everybody would say, 'Ah, thank goodness for that, now we can get some sleep...'

But that particular evening, Christmas Eve, nothing happened. All the regulars were down in the shelter: it was where we lived! We had twelve bunks, it was perhaps thirty feet square, quite spacious. If a raid was particularly heavy, there'd be people standing at the top of the steps shouting, 'Any room down there?' But usually it was the same twelve. At first we'd had a gramophone, but it had a short and inglorious life: the stylus wore out and of course you couldn't replace them. Still, we'd only had a few records and we were all sick of them anyway. There was an Elsan toilet pan surrounded only by a heavy hessian curtain. People used to time their bodily functions to coincide with bombs or gunfire or aircraft flying overhead, to give themselves a bit more privacy.

Anyway, on Christmas Eve people were saying, 'Where are they?' It got to about eight o'clock – nothing. 'Where are the buggers? What are they doing?' The evening went on into the night. Still nothing. Nobody could sleep. Someone would doze off, then wake up and say, 'Have the sirens gone?' 'No,' someone else would say, 'still nothing.' The next morning everybody was tired, because they'd hardly had any sleep. It was very unsettling, not being bombed, after all that time.

It turned out that there had been an unofficial truce. The Germans had decided to give us that night off because it was Christmas, and we had done the same to them. But I'm pretty sure it was only that one night.

Certainly on 29 December the Luftwaffe returned to London with a vengeance. In the course of that night, a hundred thousand incendiary bombs were dropped on London, accompanied by some twenty-four thousand high-explosive bombs. The famous photo of St Paul's standing unbowed among the flames dates from this night, and the fact that the cathedral survived can be credited to the extraordinary courage of the London firefighters, both regulars and volunteers.

An article in *The War Illustrated* of 17 January 1941 praised the efforts of…

… the half-dozen night porters and spotters who strove in vain to save St. Bride's; of the St. Paul's Churchyard caretakers who threw fire-bombs from the roofs of the world's most inflammable buildings, the soft goods warehouses; of the Auxiliaries – former clerks and cooks, commercial travellers and 'counter-jumpers' – who held the struggling hoses for a night and a day almost without relief in face of poisonous smoke and searing flames; of the 'Regulars' of the London Fire Brigade who darted in the fire-floats from one side of the Thames to the other in an astounding attempt to cope with a colossal outburst of flame in Southwark as well as the inferno of the City.

The article went on to refer to the old buildings, notably the premises of the 'nest of book publishers' at the corner of Ave Maria Lane and Paternoster Row, which made up 'one of the biggest of the two hundred separate fires that were at one time visible from St Paul's roof'. Another account reported the destruction of St Bride's Church and claimed that 'those who were in Fleet Street on that terrible night will not easily forget the tiered Wren steeple flaming like a monstrous torch'. St Bride's was only one of eight Wren churches that were destroyed or badly damaged. Photographs in the weekly *Hutchinson's Pictorial History of the War* showed it and St Lawrence Jewry, as well as the Great Hall of the Guildhall, 'gutted', while a picture of firemen hosing their way through burning rubble proudly announced that although the magazine's editorial offices (also in Paternoster Row) had been destroyed, 'the staff found other quarters and publication continues without a break'.

Roy in Ealing, some ten miles from St Paul's, remembers that night vividly:

We heard bombers as usual, but again there was something missing, there was no clunk of high-explosive bombs. We could hear the aircraft going round and round and no noise. My father, out of curiosity, went up to the shelter surface and thereafter I was kept in bed, but a stream of people were going up to have a look and the whole sky above London was flickering and glowing red, total saturation.

June, further away, recalls the same night:

Andover is about thirty miles from Southampton by road and much less as the crow flies; Portsmouth isn't much further. So whenever they were bombed – and they were both bombed very heavily, being such important ports – we could see the lights in the sky. One of the results of the bombing of Southampton was that some of the food stores on the docks had been destroyed, along with the meat inside them. Our supplies had to come from Derby, of all places. I remember my mother sending me to the butcher's and him telling me to come back at four o'clock that afternoon, as his supplies might have arrived by then.

The worst raids on Southampton were at the end of November and beginning of December 1940, and in Portsmouth it was January 1941, but between those two dates, just after Christmas, I remember my mother calling me to the window to 'have a look at this'. It wasn't the usual window – we were looking northeast rather than south – but I remember seeing a greeny-orange tinge in the sky. It was London burning. London was much further away than Southampton, more like fifty miles, but we could see it quite clearly. That was 29 December, the night that so much of the City was destroyed. It was a terrible time.

Roy takes up the story the morning after the fire:

My sister's husband was a volunteer fireman and he was on duty in Docklands that night. He was on the Thames fireboat *Massey Shaw*, which was quite famous. The next morning he was late home. We were all worried about him. He came in soaking wet, filthy dirty, and he sat at the table with tears running down his face. 'It was hopeless,' he said. 'There was nothing we could do.' They had been totally and utterly overwhelmed.

Later, he told us about warehouses collapsing, and sugar – molten sugar, or treacle or something – spreading across the river and virtually engulfing the boat. The heat from the burning warehouses blistered the paint on the vessel as the men tried to get their hoses turned on the buildings.

Whether the Germans did it on purpose or not, I don't know, but there was a particularly low ebb tide in the Thames that night and, with all the thousands of hoses that were trying to pump water out of it, it felt as if they had pumped the river dry. All they were doing was sucking up mud. And there was a parachute mine – about a ton of high explosives – that didn't go off but settled in the water near London Bridge, so on top of everything else the firefighters had to be careful not to disturb that until somebody came along to dismantle it. It was a truly dreadful night.

The London fires were not the only catastrophes of December 1940. Raids on Manchester and Salford were among the worst of the war, with hundreds of people killed and the Cathedral and the Royal Exchange among the buildings badly damaged. Lillian and her family were lucky – their home survived while many around them were destroyed. But a blast nearby had cut off the electricity, gas and water supplies. Lillian's brother Jack had just arrived home on leave and had planned to buy his Christmas presents at the last minute:

Jack and I walked into town to find that Market Street was roped off and firemen were busy putting out fires. Shop windows had been smashed and the contents had spewed on to the street, but the main department store, Lewis's, was open and Jack was able to do his shopping.

Our father, who was in the Home Guard, had gone out to do what he could to help and had told his colleagues about the near miss to our home. Somehow, someone produced a hamper and Dad came home with a tin of chicken, a tin of ham, even a Christmas pudding. Our windows covered with lino to create a blackout, we ate our Christmas dinner by candlelight and left the washing-up until the water supply was restored a few days later.

Millie was a young mother, also living in Manchester:

We didn't have an Anderson shelter because we lived in a terrace house with a long, thin garden. We would have had to put half of it in our garden and half in the neighbour's. Lots of people did this and shared the shelters, but my neighbour didn't want one, so that was that. Maybe he wanted the space to grow vegetables.

Instead of the Anderson shelter we had a Morrison shelter in the living room. The sides were made of wire mesh and could be lifted off or on, and there was a mattress and bedding inside. The top was very strong, to protect us in case there was an explosion and the ceiling fell in. My son and I slept in it most nights, with my baby daughter in a wicker basket on top. So any time the sirens went off I could nip out and pull her into the shelter.

That's what I did the night before Christmas Eve 1940, during what came to be called the 'Manchester Blitz'. I'd had trouble getting the children to sleep and had just dropped off myself when the sirens sounded. I staggered out of bed, grabbed the basket and pulled it into the shelter, without really waking up. A few minutes later I turned over and felt the contents of the basket crunch underneath me. It wasn't the baby's basket at all – it was the paper and string saved from last year that I was going to use to wrap presents the next day. I'd completely forgotten that I'd left it on top of the shelter so that it would be handy in the morning.

Believe me, I was wide awake by this time and able to pull my baby to safety.

Rita remembers that living near the docks in Liverpool was very frightening.

There was a lot of bombing and some people in our street were killed. I remember often being hungry. We were Catholics and used to go to Mass and Sunday school before breakfast. One Sunday just before Christmas I was walking home in the freezing cold and thinking how hungry I was – and for breakfast I had half a boiled egg.

We lived next door to a butcher's, though, so we weren't badly off for meat. I used to go and stamp the ration coupons for him and I think he must have given my mother a few extras in return. We certainly got a chicken for Christmas. The only other time we had much was when a Canadian relative of my grandmother's came to visit and he brought delicacies, like bananas and exotic sweets.

Sweets were 'on the coupon', so you could buy them, but there was never much choice – you took what you could get. I remember my grandmother exchanging coupons so that she could buy extra sweets to put in our stockings at Christmas. We were a big household – my grandmother, my parents, the three of us kids and an elderly uncle, my grandmother's brother, who had never married and lived with us. I can't imagine what my grandmother sacrificed in order to get those extra sweets.

Cardiff was also badly hit, as David remembers:

We weren't bombed every night, but we were bombed a lot – including one time very early in the New Year, which made the Christmas tree wobble. One mine destroyed six houses in a terrace only half a mile away. That was a big bang! The incendiary bombs were the real worry, because in those terraces you could walk from one house to another through the loft space, so if a fire caught hold in one a whole row could go up. I used to pick up air shells in the street on the way to school, and I remember lots of flashing in the sky. I recognised the sight and sound of the Stukas, the German dive-bombers, and I got quite good at telling the various aircraft apart. Funnily enough, I don't think I was ever frightened – I suppose I was too young really to understand what was going on.

My family weren't churchgoers: we had some Presbyterian missionaries down the road who dragged me there once or twice, but it wasn't our thing. One thing I do remember, though, is the warmth of all the neighbours. At Christmas and particularly at New Year, almost everyone would be outside in the street, wishing each other well. The atmosphere was much warmer than you get today.

Then there were surprises during a white Christmas:

We lived near Liverpool, so we had a lot of bombing and my younger brother and sister were evacuated to North Wales. I was fourteen, which I think was too old to be evacuated. So there was just my mother and me, and I had a bedroom to myself. I remember one December night, I was in bed and Mum came in and said that she'd heard guns going off. So we ran downstairs in our nighties, pulled our overcoats on and went out into the shelter in the garden. It was dark, of course, and there had been heavy snow. After a while Mum looked out and there didn't seem to be anything happening. Our neighbour must have seen us, because she called out to my mother, 'Hilda, what are you doing in the shelter? There hasn't been a siren.' 'No,' said Mum, 'but we heard the guns going off.' It turned out the crashing she'd heard was snow falling off the roof – and we'd been sitting in the shelter for about two hours for no reason at all.

In 1940, Jim, aged thirteen, who had spent the previous Christmas as an evacuee, was back home in south London with his widowed mother, his sister Ivy and Bert the lodger. He took a sardonic view of his mother's home-made gift:

The second Christmas of the war was a very austere affair, although we did celebrate the event with a roast rabbit dinner. Whilst enjoying our delicacy, churches throughout Great Britain, Germany and Italy were filled with people praying for peace, thus confusing our Lord for he failed to answer any of them... During the afternoon mother presented Bert, Ivy and me with a Christmas present, each being wrapped in some re-used brown paper. Mine was squashy, so I made a calculated guess before untying the string. I was right; it was the very balaclava I'd seen dangling from her knitting needles on many earlier occasions. I thanked her before taking it up to my bedroom, guaranteeing its safekeeping in my wardrobe drawer. Bert treated us all to a small cask of Fremlins Elephant Brand Ale, allowing me to have a shandy or two providing I asked for it.

By the end of 1943 Jim had left school and gone to work in a factory, Johnson and Phillips:

Christmas Eve fell on a Thursday in 1942, which meant we would have a long Christmas holiday; getting three clear days off was a true luxury. The management at Johnson and Phillips made it even better with the bonus of finishing work thirty minutes earlier, allowing us to have a drink with our mates... Nobody in the workshop got drunk, but a group of Charlton [football club] supporters near us did get a bit noisy singing the 'Red Red Robin' song. I took the tram home because I didn't fancy riding a bike on Christmas Eve, but disaster struck soon after I arrived indoors when I realised I had lost my wallet containing my wages and Identity card. I was not only very upset at being broke at Christmas; it was the last thing I had expected.

Mother had arranged for me to call at an address in Forest Hill to collect a chicken for our Christmas dinner. As I left with a paper carrier bag and four pence for tram fares, I was more than a little downhearted. I couldn't remember ever losing money before, and one pound, seventeen shillings and three pence was a lot of cash to lose. I knew that mother would willingly forego the contribution I made for my keep, but that didn't relieve the pain inside me. The man who sold us the chicken took me round to his back garden so he could show me the Christmas survivors, mostly those that laid eggs. He told me that he had got eight families registered with him, who he supplied with eggs as part of their food ration. He held up the chicken that was for us, to put in my paper carrier bag. It had been plucked but still retained a feathered neck and head at one end, and two yellowy orange feet at the other. The head went into the bag first and the feet stuck out of the top. Even in its undignified pose it still looked as though it was going to be a very tasty bird.

By the time I had got on the tram the chicken's head was poking out of the bottom of the bag, some moisture and a sharp beak were mainly responsible. Nobody sat next to me on the tram because my problem was gradually worsening. I was now having to carry our Christmas dinner under my arm, with its legs sticking out in front and a very bright red cone with a sunshine yellow beak dangling above the tram seat. I wasn't sorry to get home, for I feel sure some passengers were beginning to give me the bird. Ivy, Mum and Bert had smiles on their faces when I entered the living room, because a very honest gentleman had returned my wallet complete with my wages and Identity card. Mother had offered him a fair reward, but all he would say was, 'Have a Very Merry Christmas.'

In 1944 Lizzie was teaching in a London suburb:

I was staying with a cousin. We used to share a bed, and when we lay in bed and heard the doodlebugs coming she used to say to me, 'Now don't keep saying you're frightened, because I'm just as frightened as you are.' She was more placid than I was, though.

Rationing was tighter by then. My aunt – the mother of the cousin I was staying with – lived just round the corner and I remember her queuing every day for her rations and in the hope of picking up some extra treat like a tin of jam from 'under the counter'.

I did the shopping for my cousin and me, and one of our great treats was pineapple jam. Goodness knows where it came from, because there can't have been many people in Britain growing pineapples. But it was so delicious, we used to finish it long before it was time to buy any more – you were only allowed so much a week or a month. My cousin used to say, 'Don't get that pineapple jam, because it's so lovely, we'll just eat it.'

Plum or apple jam was better, because it wasn't so nice – we could make that last. But of course you had to buy what there was; you hardly ever had any choice.

We used to put a pound a week each in a pot for the housekeeping expenses. The rations cost three and elevenpence [just under 20p], and we needed a little more for bits and pieces off the rations. So of course there was quite a bit left over. My cousin got a day off every three weeks and we used to go up to London and spend what we had left in the pot. I remember just before Christmas going to Selfridges, where you could get odd things that you wouldn't find anywhere else. There was a bit of sheeting that we used to make tennis dresses: it wasn't the right time of year, of course, but you bought what you could when you could and stored it up. And there was a grey blanket with a sort of stripe at the bottom – we made a jacket out of that. Whenever we could get the materials, we did a lot of sewing and knitting, unravelling old knitting and using the wool to make other things.

When I was in Twyford at the start of the war there was another young teacher whose brother had a French wife. She used to send us magazines in French, which we tried to read. There was a lovely pattern for a jumper, with mittens and a hat. We worked out all these French instructions and made this stuff, and I've been making those mittens for friends ever since. All through the war and for years afterwards at Christmas people would ask me, 'Can you make a pair of mittens for so-and-so?' and

I did – they had a very pretty Christmas pattern with snowflakes and everyone loved them. The jumper had the same pattern, with little people in between the flakes.

The local Red Cross commandant showed us how to make sandals and slippers out of old carpet felt and that fake leather they had on the back of chairs – that was another good present. The Red Cross lady even made a pair of slippers for a bride that way.

At school we made cards and calendars out of rubbish – any leftovers from any other activity that we could make use of. We painted old strips of newspaper with powder colours to make paper chains, and more than once we had to make a dash for the shelter while we were doing it. We'd sit on benches and sing and read to the children, and if we heard a doodlebug coming we'd clap and make a bit of noise to stop them being frightened. Then we'd hear the grumbling noise of the doodlebug coming back, having dropped its bombs, and we'd think, 'Thank God, he's got someone else this time.' It was horrible, that was.

For Joan in Peterborough, Christmas 1944 was an unusual one. She had two small children already and was expecting her third at the end of January 1945:

On 15 December I went to the doctor for a check-up. The doctor was an old man who'd come out of retirement when our regular doctor was called up. After he'd examined me there was a long pause and then he said, 'I'm sorry to have to tell you you aren't pregnant at all – you have a fibroid tumour.' He gave me a letter for the midwife and I got on the bus and went to give it to her straight away. She took one look at it and at me and said, 'Fiddlesticks.' My second daughter arrived, six weeks premature, at seven o'clock that evening. She was born at home, in my bedroom, where there was no heating other than a tiny coal fire – it was freezing – and no electric light, as we had no gas or electricity upstairs. We used to take candles to light our way to bed.

Of course the baby was tiny. I remember they had to put her in a little string bag so that they could weigh her using a spring balance. She was about two and a half pounds – not much more than a kilogram.

The midwife put the baby to bed in a cot next to my bed and then she left. During the evening it seemed to me that the baby's breathing got slower and slower and I also thought she must be cold: her cot wasn't one of those cosy things you have nowadays; it was just a plain wooden-framed thing. I had a stone hot-water bottle, but she didn't; and there was only a small fire – we'd been told to put only one coal on the fire at a time, so that the room never got hotter and never got colder.

My mother had stayed to look after the other children, but by this time they were in bed and she came into my room. I said, 'I can't lie here listening to that baby – she's dying. Bring her into bed with me.' So she did, and I held her against my shoulder. In the morning the midwife said this had probably saved her life, making it easier for her to breathe. She survived and grew up to be perfectly healthy, but she did make that last Christmas of the war even more anxious than usual.

CHAPTER 3

'YOU'LL HAVE TO HAVE SHOP BUTTER FROM NOW ON'

Most people in the countryside were better fed than those in towns, not least because the more remote you were, the less impact rationing had: there always seemed to be produce available at local farms. One Liverpudlian evacuee remembered proudly struggling home for Christmas carrying a turkey from the farm where she was billeted. Travelling by train was tedious – what should have been a one-and-a-half-hour journey took five hours, with 'standing room only' the norm. Leaning against a suitcase with a turkey under her arm for five hours, she recalled, was exhausting 'but it meant that we had a decent Christmas dinner, which we wouldn't have had if we'd stuck to what we could get by handing over our coupons in the butcher's.'

Nancy was brought up in a Lincolnshire village and

trained as a teacher. When war broke out she was twenty-one and teaching in London.

This was the time of the 'Phoney War', before the worst of the bombing started, and I was allowed to travel home for Christmas. The blackout was awful – it dulled your spirits, because if you showed just a chink of light there would be the ARP [Air Raid Precautions] warden hollering at you. And it made travelling difficult: everything took longer than it was supposed to and everything was very crowded with soldiers moving about. I remember being on one train with a battalion of soldiers. They were lying on the floor because there weren't enough seats; there was smoke everywhere, because almost everyone smoked in those days, certainly the men, and you were allowed to smoke practically anywhere. You even had to climb over a few soldiers to find somewhere to stand – it was grim! There was a bit of light inside the train, but all the windows were blacked out, so you couldn't see where you were, and all the signs on the stations had been removed anyway. The driver had to call out the name of the station, or no one would have known where to get off.

One time – it was probably the following Christmas, 1940 – I was on the bus, going home from the station, and a little bus inspector got on. We all knew him – his name was Jimmy and he was about five feet tall. The bus was crowded out with people trying to get home late on a Saturday night. So Jimmy called out, 'Move down the bus. Shove down the aisle, love. Sit on anybody's knee.' And a few of us did. It was ever so dangerous, with all that over-crowding, but there were times when it was good fun too.

At home it was Mum and Dad and me, but on Christmas Day we went to my aunt's house and celebrated with her family. She always had a house full of waifs and strays – various relatives who would otherwise have been on their own. For decorations we put greenery around the pictures, and carried on much as we had done before the war. Food was no great problem in the country – we had chickens and pigs and plenty of vegetables. People talk about foraging at various times of year, for blackberries or rosehips or mushrooms, but we used to do that anyway, long before the war started.

My aunt always produced a good Christmas dinner, and we might have a glass of sherry or port. My dad and my uncle would have a beer – my uncle used to have a two-pint bottle that he kept on the floor by his chair. My aunt also managed to make fantastic puddings out of that old dried egg – she used to make dinners out of nothing, bless her heart. So we did all right. We must have had plenty to eat, because the boys used to undo the top button of their trousers, to show that they were full.

Sheila's family lived on Agar's Plough at Eton College, where her father looked after the gardens and the trees.

I had no contact with the boys there – I was at school just

65

across the river in Windsor. When an air-raid warning went off we used to head for the cloakroom, where our coats were hanging, and wrap ourselves in them, to protect ourselves against the glass if the windows were broken. It was the only shelter we had. At home we just hid under the stairs.

I remember Christmas as a happy time, but it was all very basic. We made paper chains and decorated the house with holly and ivy hung from a string. We always had a real tree, though – my father saw to that.

My mother was Irish and her relatives used to send us a goose for Christmas. There was always great discussion as to whether it was fit to eat, because it had come through the post and might have taken some days. We kept hens, though, so we could have chicken if my mother decided against the goose!

Christmas presents were basic, too. Mine were most likely to be something to wear, things that I needed anyway. But I remember embroidering tray cloths for my mother: I got them back after she died and have them to this day. When my granddaughter was setting up her own home recently I offered them to her and she said, 'Tray cloths? What are they?' How times change.

John's family also enjoyed a game bird for Christmas dinner:

My father died the year before war broke out and we were frightfully poor. I don't remember much in the way of presents. A friend used to send us a brace of pheasants, though: 'in the feather', as they say. They weren't even wrapped up – just the two birds, with address labels round their necks, sent through the post. It was very exciting when they arrived, because that was our Christmas dinner. I still enjoy pheasant to this day. Nobody drank much wine in those days – a glass of sherry before Christmas lunch was a great treat.

Hazel was ten and living in Barnstaple in North Devon:

The war didn't really touch us – Plymouth was bombed very badly and we used to hear German planes overhead going towards South Wales, but we had nothing.

We had rationing, of course, but it affected us less because we were in a small country town. My mother was a very good cook and she kept making her own jam and marmalade all through the war – she used to swap coupons with friends so that she could get more sugar. But one day she came back from our weekly market and said disgustedly, 'Well, that's it. You'll have to have shop butter from now on.' She'd always bought farm butter, but the farmers' wives no longer found it worth their while to bring their produce into town every Friday.

I also remember her going to visit a friend who had a farm and insisting that my father met her from the bus in case she tripped and dropped her basket: she'd have something ordinary like a cauliflower on the top, but hidden underneath she might have a few eggs or, if they'd killed a pig, an extra bit of bacon or pork. It wasn't anything on a large scale, but, unlike a lot of people in the cities, we were never short of food.

As far as I was concerned, Christmas during the war was much the same as it had been before and went on being afterwards. My father's unmarried sister from Newport in South Wales always came, and during the war we had another aunt living with us: her husband taught at the Duke of York's Military School, which had been evacuated from Dover to a hotel in Braunton, just a few miles from Barnstaple. So my uncle lived in the hotel and his wife lived with us, but they were part of our Christmas, too. We always had turkey – I remember my best friend at school always had goose, but I have no idea what the significance of that was. Perhaps her family knew a goose farmer... We must have had a good source of turkeys, because we also sent them to relatives in South Wales, wrapped up in brown paper. You wouldn't be allowed to do that nowadays.

There was home-made Christmas pudding, then home-made Christmas cake for tea and perhaps a game of cards. We didn't have a piano, so there was no singing, but I do remember we played a lot of cards. Some cousins would come for supper on Boxing Day and we'd have cold turkey and salad: a normal, traditional family Christmas.

Gwen had one experience that couldn't be described as traditional. She was on leave for Christmas:

My friend and I were just leaving the cinema and we

saw an elephant walking past. It turned out that there was a circus in town, but there was no performance that night, so the keepers were taking the elephant for a walk. I remember thinking he must have been pretty cold in Dorset in December.

Aldwyn turned seventeen two days before war was declared. For his family in the coal-mining valley of Rhymney in South Wales, Christmas went on much as usual, at least for the first few years:

There was a great deal of wealth there in the 1930s and the mine owners and senior officials led lives of luxury, but for the majority of the workers in the mining and ancillary businesses, living standards could be described as barely above the poverty level. My father worked for the local council, so we were somewhere in between. Budgets were tight, but we had an extremely happy childhood and I'm not aware of being in any way disadvantaged.

Our Christmas meal was like no other we'd experienced during the year. Preparations were made beforehand, the ingredients mixed for Christmas puddings, something a little special but nothing like the richness of today's products. The mixture was packed into a number of china basins and covered in cloth (from worn-out shirts or blouses, for example) and boiled in a cast-iron pan on the small gas cooker – a new acquisition only a few years before the war. Previously this would have been done on the kitchen fire, part of the cast-iron cooking range that included ovens.

As for the main attraction, the bird, my family preferred a goose. My father would have acquired it from one of the local hill farms and it was not, like today, ready prepared. Preparation was no minor undertaking. My brother had to remove all the feathers, a considerable achievement for one suffering from asthma. Some parts of the bird were discarded, but very little was wasted. The inside was cleaned after removing various organs; then it was stuffed with an inexpensive stuffing like thyme and breadcrumbs. After Christmas the remains, including the carcass, together with ample fresh vegetables (available in wartime from local farms and allotments or individual gardens) were used to produce nutritious stews for several meals. The fat was preserved (we referred to it as 'goose grease') and became a panacea for all chest and throat infections during the winter.

One thing worth mentioning about the catering is that there were no alcoholic beverages at all.

At supper the Christmas cake was produced, a fruit cake covered in marzipan and simple icing. Then there was inevitably some singing of Welsh traditional melodies and carols around the piano. One of my older sisters had trained as a teacher and specialised in music. Although my father had no formal qualifications, he was a highly respected amateur choral conductor and singing teacher.

Christmas did not end on Christmas Day. The

annual pantomime in Cardiff had its first performance on Boxing Day. Before the year ended my mother would take the younger family members to one of the performances – a very rare visit to the capital city, which in itself was an exciting event, the old steam train puffing its way down the valley. After the performance more excitement was to follow with supper at the Cosy Café in one of Cardiff's interesting arcades. The food was simple enough, but nevertheless something to be savoured – the only time throughout the year when we would be taken out for a meal.

These are some of my recollections of my childhood Christmases, and would certainly have applied to the Christmases of 1939 and 1940. Rationing began to bite a little later, but generally people managed well with the help of allotments, local farms, locally kept chickens, etc. An occasional food parcel from an aunt in America provided us with a little luxury, in the form of tinned fruit and exotic cake mixes.

Gill's family lived near Purley in Surrey, but that was dangerously close to Croydon Airport and her father was transferred to Staffordshire.

There was an enormous arms factory at a place called Swynnerton in Staffordshire, and they needed someone to run it, so after a while my father was sent there. Before the war we had had a maid, but my mother had always done the cooking and now she had to do everything herself, because the girls who had previously been 'in service' had jobs at the munitions factory.

We had a huge Christmas tree in the hall and we decorated it with things my mother had put aside over the years. Some of them I still have today, really lovely tree decorations – little birds with real feathers, all sorts of exciting things. We were supposed to help decorate it, but all I remember is accidentally knocking things off it and getting into trouble, because if anything had got broken we wouldn't have been able to replace it.

We always had an enormous turkey, which we got from a local farmer. Father was a person with friends in all societies. He was a lovely man and did a lot for other people, so there were some…shall we say, reciprocations. He also had connections with farms in Wiltshire and Devon, so we got all sorts of marvellous things that nobody else did – a brace of partridge, a brace of pheasant.

I'm sure my mother made Christmas pudding – she always managed to get things. The black market was there for people who could afford it. You were considered lucky if you could get in on it. I remember – and I can't have been more than nine or ten – hearing a programme on the radio about the black market and saying, 'Oh that's terrible, that people would do that,' and my mother said, 'Just be careful how judgemental you are.' My parents took a much more practical view than I did!

But I do remember a disaster over a Christmas cake once, when someone in the kitchen – it can't have been my mother, but perhaps it was my sister – put salt instead of sugar into the mixture. Although we'd managed to get the ingredients once, we couldn't possibly get them twice, so it was completely ruined and we didn't have a cake that year.

Even before the war, my mother never threw away anything that could be used again. I do admire her for that, because it wasn't as if she was poor, and this was long before people starting worrying about recycling. So she had a great big box of wrapping paper – lovely wrapping paper, from the days when you could get it easily. So when we were wrapping up presents, this great big box would come out. I don't think we had Sellotape – it had only just been invented, so it probably wasn't common; Mother must have had a store of ribbon, or even string, that we used to tie the parcels up.

There were always lots of people there at Christmas: we saw quite a lot of some cousins who were in the RAF and stationed nearby. Their parents lived in Harrogate, which was too far for the boys to travel, so they used to come to us. We'd go to church in the morning, then have dinner, and afterwards there were always games – silly things like hide-and-seek – and singing round the piano. I remember Christmas as a very happy time, just as it would have been if there had been no war. I don't remember ever going hungry, but looking back I realise that we were very privileged.

Less privileged were the owners of small, family-run farms. Farming was a 'reserved' occupation – like mining, engineering, teaching and a number of others, those who practised it were exempt from military service because the work they were doing at home was so important. But, as the need for fighting men increased, so the government constantly redefined the term 'reserved occupation'. A farmer might therefore find that his sons were called up, leaving him under pressure to produce more and more food to feed troops and civilians alike. This is where the Women's Land Army came in: its members were sent all over the country to help out on farms. For the first two years of the war, all the Land Girls were volunteers. Then at the end of 1941, the passing of the National Service Act allowed young unmarried women and childless widows to be conscripted into the Land Army and other female branches of the Forces; later this was extended to include women as old as forty-three. One reminiscence from Cumbria praises the Land Girls' extraordinary efforts:

> They were sent to farms where they lived and worked with the family, getting up at all hours, milking the cows, tilling the fields, enduring the cold in winter (and those winter mornings in Cumberland in unheated houses and barns were killers).

And the cows, of course, were no respecters of Christmas: they had to be milked whatever the calendar said.

Edna's clearest recollection of Christmas as a Land Girl is of digging carrots in the Suffolk frost:

> There were about twelve of us girls on this one farm.

I came from Manchester, some of the others came from Yorkshire – I think we were all volunteers, most of us in our teens, and we were sent wherever we were needed. We went home now and again – they'd give you a train ticket. We had chalets on Lady Bristow's land at Lakenheath [RAF station] and we all bunked in together. We were paid fourteen shillings [70p] a week and that was okay – we did all right on that. I really enjoyed it – they were lovely girls and I'd do it all again.

Kit's experience was even more rural. His father was attached to the Australian Navy and they had been living in Australia when he was a small child; his parents' house was let out, so when they came back at the start of the war they had nowhere to go:

Fortunately, my grandfather owned an estate in the Scottish Highlands, near the village of Kinloch Rannoch, and he let us use a cottage that was usually reserved for shooting parties. So my mother, my younger brother and I spent a year there, with my father visiting very occasionally, until we were all able to move back into our house near Portsmouth.

In one sense we were lucky, because we were well provided for. Rationing didn't really matter up there – there were rabbits aplenty and there was a farm next door where we got all sorts of things that would have been scarce if we'd lived in a town. I was five or six years old and it was my job to go to the farm each morning with a hand-held churn and collect the milk. There was also plenty of butter, eggs, and of course chickens.

But in other ways life was a bit primitive. It was bitterly cold: the cottage had no electricity or running water. We got water from the burn that ran down to the cottage and our waste went straight back into the burn – further downstream, I hasten to add. Our cooker was an ancient Rayburn that ran on anthracite – those little 'bricks' of coal that you used to get – and getting it alight was always difficult. We had an open fire in the sitting room too, so that was warm enough, but the bedrooms were freezing.

Christmas wasn't a big occasion – up in the Highlands Hogmanay was more important, and that wouldn't have involved us two little boys. One sad thing I remember about that first Christmas in Scotland was having nothing to play with: when we came back from Australia our luggage was on a separate ship, and it was sunk by an Italian submarine. So we lost the vast majority of our possessions, and the most important thing as far as my brother and I were concerned was that we had no toys. They were all somewhere at the bottom of the sea. It's fortunate that we were living where we were, because playing outside was very exciting – my mother must have wrapped us up very warmly, because we spent most of our time out of doors, and it's only in the house that I remember being cold.

Dai and Nancy grew up a few miles apart in rural Wales,

Dai on a smallholding and Nancy on a relatively isolated hill farm. Nancy remembers:

Neither of our homes had mains water or electricity until the 1960s. We both had chickens and at least one cow, so we always had eggs, milk, butter and vegetables. Some families in the area kept pigs, so there was salted pork to be had, too. Bread was made at home in big batches. Our mothers would save dried fruit and flour rations to make mince pies and Christmas pudding and cake. No wine, or any other sort of alcohol, would be in the house at any time. We looked forward to Christmas, though it wasn't massively different from the rest of the year: animals and land still had to be tended and chores completed.

I was one of ten children. We had a Christmas tree, cut from the local forestry, which we decorated with cotton wool and home-made coloured paper ornaments. We didn't go short of food in the country, and there would be a chicken and a duck for lunch. No stockings as such, but a little bag each with our names on and with an apple and some nuts and chocolate inside. The chocolate ration was something else that was saved for Christmas. I particularly remember Fry's chocolate cream and peppermint creams, but we had some ordinary chocolate too. We children would swap so that we ended up with whatever we liked best.

We had very few Christmas cards and very few presents, though I remember one time when two of my brothers were given wooden horses and made a racket playing with them on the wooden floor upstairs. And we girls had cardboard cut-out dolls with interchangeable outfits attached with tabs.

But we had to be patient on Christmas morning. My father used to read the Bible to us and pray every morning and every evening, Christmas included. We weren't allowed to look at our presents until this ceremony and breakfast were both over.

Dai remembers Christmas seeming quieter than usual in a place that was already quiet:

There were only three cars in the valley, but fuel rationing meant that even they were not seen as much. We only went to town, eight miles away, once or twice a year on the bus. But we did celebrate Christmas. We didn't have a tree but we cut a conifer branch from the local woods and decorated that. And we went out collecting holly and used that for decoration too.

There was a lady called Miss Trotter who paid for a party at the local school, and at home we would hang our stockings up downstairs and leave out a glass of milk and a mince pie for Santa Claus. I don't remember many presents, but I did get toy soldiers one Christmas and a miniature tank another. My mother played the piano and we sang carols, then there was a big football match in the village on Boxing Day.

Everything went back to normal between Christmas

Day and New Year – there weren't the long holidays there are today – but on New Year's Eve and through to midday on New Year's Day there was great excitement. That was the time for Calennig, when children would go out and sing around the neighbours and collect pennies to be shared out among them.

Gwen, from a smallholding in the same area, also remembers Calennig.

It's a Welsh tradition celebrating the New Year to which everyone looked forward. Children would sing special songs around the area and be given pennies by their neighbours. We used to make a beeline for a particular couple of houses where we knew we'd receive sixpence! All festivity had to be completed between midnight and midday.

We didn't have much money – you'd probably describe us as poor – but we had enough for food and clothes. We had plenty of milk and butter because we had a cow or sometimes two, eggs from our own chickens and enough land to be self-sufficient in vegetables. I remember every Christmas my mother sent a chicken to a relative who lived in South Wales. I had godparents in South Wales, too, and they would send presents – gloves or scarves. We might also get pencils, a rubber and clothes. One year we were given a play shop with mini packs of goods to sell: I remember that our neighbours called in, with their son, and he ate the lot.

Midway through the war Aneurin won a scholarship to the local grammar school in Aberystwyth, about twelve miles away:

There were no buses, so I had to lodge in town from Monday to Friday and take all my food for the week with me. So it was a huge treat to be home for what seemed a long time at Christmas. My father was away: he had been a builder before the war, but the Ministry of Supplies put him to work charcoal burning. Apparently charcoal was used in making explosives, so this was important war work. He was sent away to burn charcoal in Merionethshire and there was just my mother, my sister and me at home.

We had a goose from a farm in the next valley and I remember getting books from a relative in London. A local drama group would put on shows and plays, and of course Calennig was a huge treat. I had an auntie who ran a shop nearby and I suspect we got some 'extras' from her, but we could always go to local farms for produce. I don't think we experienced the shortages that people in the cities did.

CHAPTER 4

'THE EGGS TASTED OF FISH'

For most people, especially those in towns and cities, eating during the war was, quite simply, boring. There were few luxuries and little money to spend on them. With rationed goods, you registered with your local grocer, butcher and so forth, and bought what they had to sell: there was little scope for shopping around, or for visiting two supermarkets and buying your quota at both. For the housewife and mother (for in those days it was almost always she who was in charge of the shopping and the cooking), keeping the family fed was a daily challenge, requiring her to beseech friendly shopkeepers for a bit extra, and to queue endlessly for almost everything. It's hard for anyone who didn't live through it to imagine the excitement of seeing plums in the shop after a long absence, or the gloom of having to wait in a long line in order to buy the most modest quantity of tomatoes. It was said – and there was more than a little truth in it – that anyone seeing a queue outside a shop or market stall automatically joined it, hoping that when they reached the front there would still be a little of whatever was on sale to boost the weekly rations.

Food rationing didn't begin until 1940, so from that point of view Christmas 1939 didn't differ much from the Christmases that had gone before. In *Good Housekeeping* magazine's cookery pages, a 1939 article headed 'The Festive Roast' gave no indication that turkey would be in short supply; it suggested eking out the poultry with a 'lavish quantity' of sausages or ham and adding a few mushrooms or the liver of the bird to veal stuffing – and gave a recipe for chestnut stuffing that included sausage meat, without suggesting that any of these things might be remotely profligate. But the following year was, of all those in the war, the one of greatest change – from more or less normality to considerable deprivation. In 1940, *Good Housekeeping*'s cakes were decorated with 'oddments out of the store cupboard' and the accompanying text contained expressions such as 'as near the traditional as possible' and 'a cake that will keep well and taste good but not be extravagant'. In the same year, *Woman's Weekly* decorated its Christmas cake with desiccated coconut and a few marshmallows, while *Woman's Own* made a virtue out of necessity:

Do you know, I wouldn't be a bit sorry if this Christmas wakes up the people who have never associated this merry season with anything but food... After all, who's to say you can't make merry as well on stuffed rabbit as stuffed turkey?

Roy in Ealing, whose parents ran a hardware shop, remembers big changes between those two Christmases, when he was nine and ten:

Christmas [1940] was approaching, but this was hardly a season of goodwill to all men. We could think of a few exceptions!

It was to be a very austere occasion. Mum was fretting about what she could organise for Christmas dinner. Then one day Dad came in, swinging a dead rabbit by its ears. We never did find out where he got it from, although we knew he had a friend who was a bit of a poacher.

Mum was horrified. 'What have you got there?' she said. 'I'm not skinning that thing! You'll have to do it.' Dad was a bit squeamish about it, too, so eventually he took it down to the local butcher and got him to do it in exchange for a big chunky bar of carbolic soap from the shop. So we had a skinned rabbit, and that was our Christmas dinner.

A few days earlier, to our surprise, Mum had announced, 'I'm going to make a cake.' We all looked at each other. 'A what… what with?' Dad exclaimed.

Not being involved, I have no idea of the ultimate ingredients, but I do know that carrots, powdered egg and National Wholemeal breadcrumbs featured strongly. It certainly looked good. Taste? Well, debatable is the word, but we scoffed the lot.

In 1941 *Good Housekeeping* was driven to suggesting 'Cakes without eggs': the various alternative ingredients included baking powder (for lightness and raising properties) and specially produced and marketed 'egg substitutes' containing dextrin or 'British gum', to mimic the coagulant properties of eggs. There were also recipes for fresh-salted cod, which came from Iceland and was billed as 'a welcome addition to our food supplies at a time when fresh fish is scarce'. Recipes for 'Creamed Cod with Tomatoes', 'Curried Cod Hot-pot' and 'Baked Cod au Gratin' (which required an ambitious 2–3 ounces of grated cheese – all of an adult's weekly ration and more – and a little grated onion, if available) show just how tightly belts had been drawn in.

The first foods to be rationed – in January 1940 – were bacon, butter and sugar. All meat was rationed in March, tea and margarine in July. A number of other foods, including eggs, were added to the list in 1941, and packets of powdered egg began to be imported from the USA the following year. Each packet contained the equivalent of twelve eggs, and adults were entitled to one packet every four weeks in addition to their 'shell eggs'. (Children got two packets, because eggs were seen as 'body-builders' and the powdered egg made up for shortages in other protein-rich foods such as cheese, meat and fish.)

The Ministry of Food carefully referred to 'shell eggs'

rather than 'fresh eggs', anxious to sell the public on the idea that dried eggs were every bit as good: 'Nothing is added. Nothing but the moisture and the shell taken away, leaving the eggs themselves as wholesome, as digestible and as full of nourishment and health-promoting value as if you had just taken the eggs new laid from the nest.' Powdered egg was easy to use – you simply mixed one tablespoon of powder with two tablespoons of water to reconstitute the equivalent of one 'shell egg' – but whatever its nutritional value, it made for a lumpy omelette with a nasty powdery aftertaste. The fact that Roy in Ealing remembers scrambled powdered egg as a Friday-night treat is another indication of how thriftily most city-dwellers were living.

In addition to these basics that could be purchased only if you had the requisite coupons, other foods were bought from an allocation of points – twenty-four per adult every four weeks. This list included rice (eight points per pound), dried fruit (from eight to sixteen points per pound), tinned sardines (two points per tin), plain biscuits and rolled oats (both two points per pound).

In its eagerness to promote good nutrition, the Ministry of Food created campaigns featuring the cartoon characters Doctor Carrot – 'the children's best friend' who, with his high vitamin A content, would help you to see in the blackout – and Potato Pete, who sang a little song encouraging everyone to enjoy potatoes in every form, 'including chips, remembering spuds don't come in ships'.

Throughout the nation, even in the smallest urban spaces, people took to growing vegetables in response to another campaign, 'Dig for Victory'. It wasn't just back gardens that were converted into vegetable patches – public parks, swathes of Kew Gardens and the moat at the Tower of London were called into service, too. Schoolchildren had 'gardening lessons' or were encouraged to volunteer to work in local allotments – one Dorset man remembered being paid fourpence (less than 2p) an hour to pick potatoes.

There were special rations for pregnant women and for small children: Cadbury's even promoted their milk chocolate under the slogan 'Children first, please': 'All the food value of the milk is in it – a glass and a half in every half-pound. Supplies are limited but are being distributed fairly in the areas we supply. When your turn comes, please remember that growing children need this extra refreshment most.' Advertisements for Nestlé's Milk took the same line: 'Now that supplies are short, shouldn't we – the rest of us – leave the grocer's limited stocks of Nestlé's Milk for those anxious mothers who have delicate babies to feed?'

In the absence of basics such as meat and eggs, the use of 'mock' recipes became widespread. The index of one recipe book lists:

- *Mock apricot flan, with a filling of grated carrots, almond essence and plum jam*
- *Mock crab, made from margarine, dried eggs, cheese, salad dressing and vinegar*
- *Mock cream, with margarine and sugar added to milk and dried milk powder*
- *Mock duck – sausage meat, apples, onions and herbs*

- *Mock goose – similar to mock duck but with potatoes rather than sausage meat (in other words, with no meat at all)*
- *Mock marzipan – margarine, almond essence, sugar or golden syrup and soya flour*
- *Mock oyster pudding, containing soft roe*
- *Mock oyster soup – primarily fish trimmings, vegetables, herbs and spices*
- *Mock whipped cream – cornflour, milk, margarine, sugar and vanilla essence*

At Christmas 1942 the Ministry of Food published an advertisement thanking people for their loyalty and helpfulness in recognising that 'good living' must now mean 'healthy living'. It gave recipes for a Christmas Pudding that included carrot and potato; Christmas Fruit Pies, 'a good alternative to mincemeat', containing prunes and stale cake crumbs; and 'Emergency Cream' made from warm water, margarine, household milk powder, sugar and vanilla. Very much the best anyone could do under the circumstances, but they must have made for a dull eating experience.

Middle-class women had been dealt another body blow with the coming of war: for the first time, they had to do their housework – including cooking – themselves. Between 1901 and 1951 the number of servants in the UK halved from 1.5 million to 750,000, at a time when the population increased from 38.3 million to 50.3 million. In other words, the percentage of the population in domestic service decreased from just under 4 per cent to just under one and a half. The main reason was that when war broke out, women were called away or volunteered to do essential work in factories, on the land and in the armed forces, and never came back to their pre-war posts.

Perhaps surprisingly, many women who had had servants before the war seem to have been able to work miracles in the kitchen. Gill quoted her father as saying, 'Your mother is a magician', because 'it didn't matter how dire the situation was food-wise, she was a brilliant cook and what bits and pieces she could pick up always ended up being a feast.' On the other hand, Wendy had no detailed recollection of Christmas dinners during her wartime childhood and put this down to her mother *not* having been a brilliant cook. Before the war she had had a live-in 'maid of all work'; once that woman left for a job in a factory, Wendy's mother had to 'make do' with three domestic helps – married women who lived out. She was immensely house-proud and, when the authorities questioned whether she needed three helpers, she was adamant that she did. However, she did the cooking herself and never quite got the hang of it.

So, with all the restrictions in place, how did people manage to produce a celebratory meal at Christmas? The truth is that a lot of them didn't. Many remembered Christmas as being 'just the same as any other day' – they might have gone to church in the morning, but that was the only difference.

Susan's father was employed at a working men's club in Kent and struggled to make ends meet. The only thing she remembers doing to 'celebrate' Christmas is writing to some of the young members of the club who were serving overseas:

Writing to an Army Postal Services address was free, so it was a small thing we could do to remind old friends that there were people at home thinking of them. But as for Christmas dinner, there was no question of that. Very occasionally – I remember this happening about three times during the war, not necessarily at Christmas – the butcher would have some sausages, which we could cook in a little gas oven in the club's kitchen. If we could persuade the baker to part with a little extra bread, we could hand out perhaps half a sausage in half a slice of bread (no butter, of course) to each person. That was a real treat.

Joan in Suffolk remembers her Christmases being equally frugal, recalling that 'Mum and Dad had a tot of rum in their tea on Christmas morning; it was the only time they drank, and the only thing they did as a Christmas celebration.'

Others, particularly those with children, did make an effort. This might involve saving up coupons (and perhaps doing without meat or butter or sugar) for weeks or months; it might involve bartering, or getting a bit extra under the counter, or just making the best of what you had.

For many people, chicken was a once-a-year Christmas treat. Usually this meant a cockerel that had been fattened up for the purpose, or a hen that had got too old to lay eggs. One woman recalled her mother winning a chicken in a raffle and having a disconcerting experience, saying 'She had to pluck it herself and when she came to take its innards out she could feel the eggs still inside it.'

In Ros's family, as in many others, a little had to go a long way:

We kept chickens and had them as a treat; we certainly had chicken for Christmas dinner, but only tiny bits: my uncle and aunt and cousin Christine came from next door, so there would have been at least six of us and sometimes other relatives too. That meant there wasn't much to go round. I remember one time when I was given a leg, I was over the moon. Even though I was an only child, I was always taught to share, and to get an entire leg to myself was amazing.

My mother was very strict about sharing. There was one time when I won a banana in a charity raffle – that was a real thrill, because we hardly ever saw bananas – and my mother made me share it with Christine. I ended up with about two bites, so either it was a very small banana or Christine got a lot more than her fair share.

Potatoes on Christmas Day I remember well – we grew them – and I think we had cabbage. But we didn't have mincemeat, so there were no mince pies. Christmas cake was a joint venture between my mother and aunt. Families and neighbours used to get together and pool coupons, so that they could buy bigger quantities of sugar and eggs and so on. We didn't have drinks cupboards back then, and my mother didn't approve of alcohol anyway. But if we were lucky she would put a little drop of brandy in the pudding: I was in my teens by the end of the war, and old enough to know that this was a bit daring. We were allowed brandy and sherry in the house because they were medicinal.

After Christmas dinner my mother and my aunt and my aunt's sister used to do the washing-up. I was very jealous, because I knew they were having a conversation and I would have liked to be in on it, but I was told I was too young. They used to get into the kitchen and be there practically all afternoon. The washing-up couldn't have taken that long.

My father worked for the Ministry of Food and got to be the deputy head for our area. In fact, the top man was discovered to be fraudulent, so for a while my father was the head. Our local grocer obviously thought Dad was worth keeping in with and he was forever offering my mother extra bits of this and that – more than she was entitled to on the ration – or things like sultanas, which were in very short supply. But my mother would never accept anything. And it wasn't tiny amounts: you could usually get a handful of sultanas, but he was offering her half a kilo or so. I remember it so clearly – there was a scene in the shop when she said, 'No. Put it away! I don't want it.' This was typical of her – just as she was fierce about sharing, she was adamant about not taking more than her fair share. But it did mean we couldn't make a proper Christmas cake.

It must have been the first or second winter of the war when my mother complained that the previous year she'd made three or four cakes and given them away as presents. This year she had what she called a 'derisory' quantity of fruit and nuts – I always remember that, because I'd never heard the word before and had to ask what it meant – and could barely scrape together the ingredients for one cake. She cut the currants and sultanas into quarters and sliced a few dates as small as they would go in order to make the cake look darker.

After that, I think we just had a sponge, with powdered egg and margarine. I had to whisk it by hand, which was really difficult in the days before electric beaters. My mother used to pretend that whisking the cake was an honour, but I hated it. I'm sure I never had a real Christmas cake until after the war.

It wasn't just from the grocer that Mum wouldn't accept things. There was a time, when I might have been twelve or thirteen, that we had two Canadian soldiers billeted on us at Christmas time. They were lovely and had access to all sorts of wonderful things – bread, biscuits, even toffees. My mother wouldn't accept anything from them either, but I did, and two or three toffees made all the difference to my Christmas that year.

Sam was born just a year before war broke out and, according to family legend, lay in his pram looking up at the sky where the Battle of Britain was raging. His mother used to maintain that just about the first words he uttered were, 'It's one of ours.' His maternal grandparents lived in the same street as him and his parents and sister – 'We were at number 31 and they were at number 7.' The extended family used to celebrate together, and they *did* have mince pies:

It was down to my mother to make the mince pies. We had about four or five trays with those individual holes in them – some of them were cupcake size and some of them were round – we spent a lot of time making mince pies. We used ready-made mincemeat – you could get it at Christmas, in limited quantities. They all went in the oven at number 31, and I remember the wonderful smell of them cooking; then they were taken solemnly, with a cloth over them, to number 7, where the main Christmas celebration took place.

I remember the pudding being steamed, too, in an earthenware bowl with a cloth round it. We were allowed to put a finger into the batter and taste it, 'to help make the pudding'. Once some of my cousins were there and my uncle gave all us children a threepenny bit to stir into the mix. We had to make a wish as we stirred it in; then whoever found a coin in their portion of pudding on Christmas Day got to make more wishes. I'm sure we all wished for the war to be over and an extra helping of pudding – not necessarily in that order.

My grandparents had various fortified wines – sherries and ports, I suppose – but they were never purchased: they were all left over from previous years when there wasn't rationing. So in the course of the war the grown-ups gradually went through my grandparents' drinks cupboard.

Being the only grandson, and my grandmother's pet, I was allowed to have the odd sip of something or other, and also the odd cigarette, or part of it. My grandmother liked Turkish cigarettes – the ones that were squashed – and I was allowed the occasional puff.

Although many people talk about silver threepenny bits in the Christmas pudding, the last of these was minted in 1941 (except for use in the West Indies, where they were issued until 1944). The coin was replaced by a larger twelve-sided brass one, which remained in use until Britain 'went decimal' in 1971. There was great excitement – and a wish to be made – if you found a coin in your portion, but most families handed them back to mother or grandmother, to be washed and used again next year.

Joan in Peterborough also had her parents living nearby:

My father kept chickens, so we usually had a chicken for Christmas dinner – my parents always came to me on Christmas Day. Dad also had an allotment, which supplied us with fresh vegetables. We got extra eggs from my father, and kept them in the pantry in a big crock with some fishy stuff called isinglass dissolved in water. Isinglass is used in beer-making now, but in those days we bought it in tins and used it to keep eggs fresh. If you relied on what you were allowed on the ration, you had only one egg a week each, and at bad times one a fortnight.

Because I had small children the Infant Welfare

provided me with orange juice and cod liver oil. The orange juice came from America, so that didn't start until 1941 or so. I also had extra rations from the Women's Voluntary Services, a charity that organised food for those in need. At Christmas they gave me a gift food parcel from America that included a big tin of ham. Covered in home-made pastry, it made a lovely pork pie for Boxing Day. And with four ration books – mine, my husband's and my children's – we got enough dried fruit to make a Christmas cake and enough sugar for me to ice it. We lived next door to the Co-op shop and the people there occasionally had dried fruit, dates, nuts and even oranges – these were all in short supply, but they helped to fill the stockings which we put on the children's beds on Christmas Eve. If ever we saw anyone coming out of the Co-op looking as if they had more shopping than usual, we'd rush in to see if we could get it, too.

In the latter part of the war my husband worked as a lorry driver for the NAAFI – the Navy, Army and Air Force Institutes, which ran cafes, shops, clubs and other entertainment for people in the services. He delivered food to various camps and was able to bring home the odd treat. Sometimes it was jelly or blancmange (we seemed to eat a lot of blancmange during the war and I've never liked it since); sometimes it was a few chocolate wafers in bars like a KitKat. I remember having a sort of Christmas party for my son's friends; I broke the chocolate into fingers and gave a bit to all of them. They were very excited: we hardly ever had chocolate and they had never seen chocolate wafers before.

Rita in Northampton remembers Christmas as fairly quiet:

The family used to get together and pool ration books so that we could have a decent meal, but it wasn't the big celebration that it is today. Nobody could afford the sort of things we take for granted nowadays. By 'the family' I mean my mum's sister and her mother; Grandma kept chickens and she used to supply one for our Christmas dinner. I think we had potatoes, carrots, cabbages – nothing very special – and perhaps an apple pie. Then we used to go to my other nan's for a cup of tea.

Drink was hard to come by: a lot of those who liked a tipple made their own wine – from dandelions, rhubarb, even potatoes. A few of the grown-ups would get three sheets to the wind on that. I remember lying in bed upstairs and hearing cork after cork popping – you'd have thought it was a machine gun going off!

Mum drove a petrol tanker all over the country and one of the places she delivered to was an American base: the Americans always seemed to be able to get anything and Mum would sometimes come home with a few sweets for us, and once even a pair of nylon stockings for herself! Once she managed to get me a big slab of chocolate – but it was dark chocolate and I didn't like it. She was so thrilled to be able to give me such a special present that I didn't want to disappoint her: I tried to eat it and be thrilled too, but it was hard.

Beryl was born in 1940 and lived in Hillingdon, Middlesex:

I remember my mother plucking the chicken for Christmas dinner in the kitchen, presumably because it was too cold to do it outside; she used to put the feathers in a old tin bath. We had a proper bathroom, but my mother used this tin bath to carry the clothes out to the washing line and it ended up full of feathers. I also remember my father cutting the neck off the chicken and drawing it, and my mother making gravy out of the giblets – that was a real treat, to have a chicken and gravy at Christmas.

David in Cardiff also remembers chickens having to be 'dealt with':

We lived in a street of terraced houses and there was a baker's-cum-cake shop on the corner. At Christmas, everyone in the street used to take their fowls there for roasting: we had a small oven at home, but of course the bakery had a huge one. They would steam our puddings, too.

Chicken was the main fare at Christmas. Occasionally we had goose, which I've never had since, though my memory is that I liked it. We kept the odd chicken and I remember Dad cutting the head off one and it running round the garden for fully ten minutes. Very frightening!

We must have kept our chickens to eat, because we got eggs from a neighbour across the street. Unfortunately, he fed his chickens on fishmeal, so the damned eggs tasted of fish, too.

Making use of a baker's oven was widespread – and could be a bit precarious, as Maureen in Suffolk remembers:

We fattened up a cockerel for Christmas dinner, but it was too big to go in our oven, so Dad used to take it down the hill to the baker's on the front of his bike: not in a basket, just the cockerel in a roasting tin, balanced on his handlebars. The baker's had a bigger oven, so they cooked it for us. They also made the gravy and Dad used to bring that back in a milk can.

Despite the shortages and the strict rationing, there were always those who could get round the system. Brenda from Stockton remembers an unorthodox way of acquiring Christmas dinner:

Word went round that one of the local allotment keepers was killing a pig and a joint of pork was promised. It arrived one Friday evening – a knock on the door and a loud thump as the pork was dropped on the mat. The local black market at work!

Colin's family came by their pork in a more civic-minded way:

> We were living in Watford and there were a whole lot of pig clubs in town: one of them had eighteen pigs. My mum belonged to one and every morning when she went shopping – because you did go food shopping every morning in those days, buying fruit and veg and bread fresh every day – she would collect up the kitchen scraps, take them with her and drop them off in the bin outside the piggery. The scraps would be boiled into a mush and fed to the pigs, which would be fattened up for Christmas. So all the members of the club got a lovely joint of pork for their Christmas dinner.

Producing 'all the trimmings' wasn't too difficult, as there was rarely a shortage of potatoes, or of winter vegetables such as sprouts, cabbage and cauliflower. But Jack, aged five and living in Nottingham, remembers an argument about potatoes:

> There was a broadcast every morning on the wireless from the 'Radio Doctor', advising us on how to keep healthy during the war. I remember he recommended boiling potatoes in their jackets, as that stopped the vitamin C escaping and getting lost in the cooking water. My grandmother, who was a country lass, was appalled by this and absolutely vetoed it for Christmas dinner: she called potatoes in their skins 'pig taters', as

they were part of what they had fed to the pigs when she was a girl.

Ivan in Suffolk remembers a treat for Christmas breakfast:

Cold rabbit pie. It would be cooked two days before, so that at the bottom there was lots of nice jelly. Pastry on the top, jelly on the bottom – that was one of the main things for the country people for Christmas Day breakfast. I don't know anybody who didn't have it.

Making the Christmas pudding was a family affair, as Tony recalls:

A couple of weeks before Christmas it was all hands on deck to make the Christmas pudding. There was a bottle of stout, currants which you'd had to save up, then Mum would peel the carrots and we'd have to grate them and stir it all in. Once the Americans came over there was sort of a NAAFI above Woolworths. Their families and the American authorities would send tins of pineapple and peanuts and things like that that we hadn't been able to get. And there'd be mixed fruit, with currants, sultanas and nuts in it, in a tin. So we were able to get dried fruit, which had been in short supply before that.

Albert remembers another sort of pudding:

We had Christmas pudding at lunchtime, then for tea

we'd have trifle. My mother would have jam sponge – home-made cake and home-made jam – broken up into chunks, and she'd pour a bit of sherry on it. Then she'd spread custard over it – I think we had Bird's custard powder – and cream on the top. But the cream was the 'top of the milk', because this was in the days before homogenised or semi-skimmed or anything of that sort: there was always an inch or two of fairly thick cream that settled at the top of a bottle of milk. But whipping it to make it spreadable was a lot of work.

Mabel, writing from Coventry to her husband in Egypt on Christmas Day 1942, also extolled the virtues of trifle:

We had a cockerel and a piece of pork for dinner, & of course pudding & sauce. I, as usual, made all the preparations & cooked the dinner, & I've made a nice 'sloshy' trifle for tea. I hope I don't make you too envious, but I thought you would like to know what we are doing & having. You may rest assured, darling, that we are keeping the things by us to make you the grandest, sloshiest trifle you ever had in your life. In fact we only had two jellies by us & were saving them for you and Cyril, but your Mum gave me one last weekend so we went all mad & used one for today!

The Christmas cake was something else that required initiative and compromise. Joyce from Suffolk remembers:

If we had any fat left over from the joint, then that

would go in the cake, if we didn't have enough butter or margarine. But Mother used to make something called a vinegar cake – you put a spoonful of vinegar in instead of an egg and it had some chemical reaction that made it lighter. We had eggs because we kept chickens, but maybe she was saving the eggs for something else.

Ivy lived in Leeds with a grandmother who took a no-nonsense approach to wartime cookery:

Whoever first said that necessity was the mother of invention must have been thinking of rationing – and of my grandmother. She took the view that we had to get on with it, and that's what she did. Egg rationing made conventional cake-making well nigh impossible, so Gran made a Christmas cake where bicarbonate of soda replaced the eggs:

4oz grated carrot
2 tablespoons golden syrup
3oz caster sugar
4oz margarine
1 teaspoon bicarbonate of soda
6oz mixed dried fruit
½ teaspoon vanilla essence
½ teaspoon almond essence
12oz sifted self-raising flour
1 teaspoon ground cinnamon
about 6 fl oz warmed milk

- *Preheat the oven to 220°C/425°F/gas mark 7.*
- *In a small pan and over a low heat, cook the carrot and syrup for a few minutes, stirring continuously so that it doesn't burn or stick. Remove from the heat and set aside.*
- *Cream the sugar and margarine in a bowl until light and fluffy. Stir the bicarbonate of soda into the carrot and syrup mixture, then add to the sugar and margarine.*
- *Add the dried fruit and essences and stir, then fold in the flour and cinnamon. Add enough warmed milk to make the mixture hold together but remain soft and moist.*
- *Turn the mixture into a deep, greased and lined 7in round cake tin. Level the surface, then make a deep hole in the centre with a spoon to stop the cake from rising too much.*
- *Place in the oven, then immediately turn the temperature down to 150°C/300°F/gas mark 2. Bake for three hours, checking occasionally that the surface isn't burning. If it is, cover it with foil or strong brown paper.*
- *Turn out and cool on a wire rack, then store in an airtight container.*

With so little dried fruit available, the carrots kept the cake moist. Gran also used to make a sort of marzipan using semolina, a little icing sugar and almond essence. Traditional 'royal' icing using egg whites and icing sugar was out of the question. A substitute could be made using sugar and dried milk, but it was hardly the same.

Lack of ingredients generally encouraged resourcefulness. Adding grated raw apple and cooked apple pulp to mincemeat made it go further. If mincemeat simply wasn't available, grated apple became the principal ingredient, with the addition of as much spice and dried fruit as people could lay their hands on. Ivy continues:

> Gran added grated potato to her pastry – it made the pastry lighter and eked out the fat ration. The Ministry of Food was always encouraging us not to eat too much fat, not that there was much chance of that!

Grated carrot and potato helped with the Christmas pudding, too:

> 1 cup flour
> 1 cup breadcrumbs
> 1 cup sugar
> ½ cup suet
> 1 cup mixed dried fruit
> 1 teaspoon mixed spice
> 1 cup grated carrot
> 1 cup grated potato
> 1 level teaspoon bicarbonate of soda dissolved in
> 2 tablespoons hot milk
>
> Mix the flour, breadcrumbs, sugar, suet, fruit and spice together in a bowl, then add the carrot and potato. Mix well. Add the bicarbonate of soda and milk, mix to combine, and turn into a well-greased pudding basin. Boil or steam for four hours.

Maureen, aged about seven, remembers a distressing experience with Christmas cake ingredients:

> We had a wireless that ran on an accumulator, and the local garage used to charge it for us. I remember one Christmas my mother said, 'If you're really good and go up and get the accumulator, I'll give you a special treat.' I went up to the garage wondering what she was going to give me, because I knew that one of my brothers who was in the Forces had sent a parcel home. I carried the accumulator very carefully: it was made of glass with lead plates inside, so it was heavy and I knew if I dropped it, it would break and I'd be in trouble. I got it safely home and asked Mum for my treat. She went into the pantry and brought out this peel. All sorts of different peel, orange peel, lemon peel, to put in a Christmas cake – my brother had sent it from abroad and I've never tasted anything so disgusting. I was so upset: I'd thought I was going to be given a chocolate or a sweet or something.

Even after chicken and Christmas pudding, there was likely to be a substantial tea later in the day. Ursula remembers paying the price for gluttony:

> The Americans sent things in tins, like Spam. When we had Spam, that was a big day out! We had Spam and salad for tea on Christmas Day, so Mum must have thought it was a treat. Salad was quite easy to come

by, because it grew in England. Whatever else we went without, I don't remember there ever being a shortage of lettuce. But even if they weren't formally rationed most things were in short supply, because so much food was sent out to the Forces. If you got an egg, it had to go three ways. And we hardly ever saw butter – it was all margarine, which I hated.

One Christmas Eve my mother went out shopping and left me in the house alone. I must have been about twelve. I was hungry and thought she wouldn't miss a piece of bread. But it was that National Wheatmeal Loaf that was meant to be good for you, but looked dirty and beige and horrible. I needed something to put on it. I went into the larder, saw what I thought was butter, shoved it inch-thick on the bread and ate it. And was I sick! It wasn't butter at all, it was margarine and it had a foul taste. I certainly paid for that thievery. I should have realised that we wouldn't have had a great chunk of butter in the larder, but I must have assumed it was there as a Christmas treat and was too hungry (or greedy) to care that I shouldn't be helping myself to it.

Careful housewives had to guard against such pilfering – and other accidents. Dorothy remembers:

We had two big apple trees in the garden and very often gave away extra fruit to neighbours. We all gave up sugar in our tea and coffee and saved our sugar to make jam. I remember my mother dissolving a lot of sugar in water in the kitchen sink ready to make some preserves, which she would give away as Christmas presents. My dad came in from working in the garden, not realising, and washed his hands in it. I heard my mother scream, but it was too late – that was several weeks' worth of sugar literally down the drain.

Eking things out was tough and, for those who adhered strictly to the rationing rules, they would only get tougher. But by the time the Americans joined the war at the end of 1941, the code-breakers of Bletchley Park were regularly deciphering German messages, making the blockades in the Atlantic less effective. More convoys were getting through, and the ships that were supplying American Forces in Britain and the rest of Europe sent almost forgotten luxuries. American soldiers were also paid much more than their British counterparts – one estimate says an average of five times as much. To Brits who had endured two years of privation, it didn't seem as if the Americans were short of anything. Certainly there were good things to be had if you knew the right people, as Vera remembers:

My stepfather was in the Merchant Navy; he was back and forth to America all the time and he always used to bring stuff home. I remember Cadbury's Dairy Milk at Christmas, proper bars of it, not just the square or two that most people had. So we did alright. We lived near Aintree in Liverpool and there was the Hartley's jam factory and a biscuit factory nearby. Everybody who worked there used to be given so much every month and a bit more at Christmas, so if you were matey with them you sometimes got some of their extras.

Bridget was a small child in rural Norfolk when the RAF base at North Pickenham was taken over by the USAAF in 1944. The 'luxuries' they introduced included Heinz baked beans and chewing gum:

Just outside the village the Americans had a refuse dump and we children used to go scavenging there, particularly looking for bars of chocolate, Mars bars, some unopened... The amount of waste was phenomenal and we were grateful for the stuff that they were throwing away [...]

The children of North Pickenham and the surrounding villages were invited to a Christmas party held on the base. The Americans were kind and generous. We had never seen so much food in our lives, and it probably did not suit us eating so much after scarce rations. When my aunt came to collect me she was appalled to see food on the floor and sugar scattered about.

Brenda was another who benefited from the Americans' generosity:

One year we received an invitation to a Christmas party at the Burtonwood Air Base. My father worked for the Air Ministry and the base was mainly occupied by American airmen. No expense was spared – food, boxes of sweets and a big present delivered by Santa who arrived in a helicopter. I remember the bars of chocolate, names we hadn't heard of – Baby Ruth bars and Hershey bars. I visited the USA for the first time when I retired and it took a bit of searching to find the American chocolate bars I remembered.

Mavis remembers an oddity:

I was eight in 1942, the first year there were Americans at the local air base. I still believed in Father Christmas, but only just – my twin sister had told me that it was Daddy dressed up, but I didn't want to believe her, and I suspect she didn't want to believe it either. When we were invited to a party at the American base and discovered that Father Christmas had an American accent – which we recognised from Disney films we had seen at the cinema – we were more confused than ever.

For Matthew, a pupil of the Foundling Hospital Schools in Berkhamsted, the Americans brought unimagined luxury:

When we were about eleven or twelve, the Americans would come over, in 1943 that would have been, and there were some big air stations near Berkhamsted, and…they got hold of the school and they said, 'We'd like to take as many of your children as you'll let go to our army base' – because they were called the US Army

Air Force – 'and we'll give 'em a treat.' So they sent their lorries over and they picked us up, and we were given how to behave, you know, and they absolutely spoiled us rotten […] We were all sick because we couldn't handle the stuff. The food and the presents and the kindness of these people, it was absolutely staggering…

Sam, from the same school, remembers a similar occasion:

We used to go to the local aerodrome at Bovington where the Yanks were; we used to all go down there for Christmas and they used to give us presents and feed us with all this rich food, you know, which we'd never seen before. We had turkey and cranberry jelly, and I was sick, it was too rich! I remember that vividly.

June in Andover didn't benefit directly from the Americans' generosity, but managed to celebrate anyway:

There were lots of Americans in our area and they gave lovely parties, but only for the younger children. I was at secondary school and we had to make do with what we could arrange for ourselves. We had concerts at school, and we were lucky in that, in addition to a domestic science lab, we had our own kitchen with a proper cook – a very good cook, who managed to squeeze our rations into something really nice. I remember in 1944 for some reason there had been an extra off-ration issue of dried fruit, so she was able to make proper Christmas puddings. And one time all the butchers in town had an issue of oxtail. That was really lovely – once you'd eaten the meat you could use the bones to make soup. There was plenty of it, too – it must have fed the whole town for two weeks.

Doreen was twelve when war broke out, an only child living in Edinburgh, where her father ran a marble and granite business:

My father knew a lot of tradesmen, butchers among them, who at Christmas and New Year would give us chicken, rabbit and turkey, the latter being used more for Hogmanay celebrations. It had been cooked before it reached us and was looked on as a Hogmanay treat, to which other family members – uncles and aunts – were invited…

Apart from the above-mentioned items in the poultry category, food did become drearier as the Christmas times went on, but I remember one highlight. After the USA came into the war we received a food parcel from the Washington Monumental Company in Spokane. My father must have had some business connection with them. There were some printed Christmas carols and Betty Crocker cake mix. The latter seemed very exotic to us, as we had been trying fatless sponges with powdered egg, which had to be consumed the same day, as they went hard. My mother would have liked more tins of Spam. Strange as it might seem now, Spam proved a great innovation, not only at Christmas but throughout the year.

Kay was living in Glasgow:

I don't think we ever went hungry: my father had an allotment, so we had all the potatoes, cauliflower, anything like that, that we wanted. And because my grandparents came from farming stock they were able to send us things that probably they shouldn't have – rabbits, chickens, occasionally a salmon, which would certainly have been poached. Any bones or leftover bits would have been made into soup – my mother always managed something. I also remember once my grandparents sent us a lump of pork, carefully wrapped up in dock leaves and hidden inside an old settee. This must have been in case anyone inspected them – they would have said they were sending us the settee because we had lost ours in the bombing, or something – but that was how we got our Christmas dinner that year.

Having said that, we certainly didn't have much in the way of presents – I remember once I was given a clock made out of icing, and that was it.

Rationing wasn't the only way of keeping an eye on the food supply: farmers had to get a licence to slaughter animals, even for their own use. One farmer's daughter remembers:

My aunt, uncle and four cousins were coming for

Christmas dinner, so Dad slyly (and illegally) killed and butchered two pigs. He would have been planning to salt a lot of it: it lasted ages that way. He asked my brother to hang two sides in the barn for the local policeman to inspect and to stash the others away. It was only as he was showing the policeman into the barn that he realised my brother had hung up two right-hand sides – anybody could see they must have come from two different pigs.

I guess the policeman wasn't the son of a butcher or a farmer. He certainly didn't have a suspicious mind. He counted two sides, filled in his form and went away happy. We had the most lavish Christmas dinner I can remember during the war – and plenty of bacon for months afterwards.

It wasn't just food that was in crisis, of course. Clothes and material suffered as well. British clothes manufacturers increased production, particularly at the 'haute couture' end of the market, when the fall of France in 1940 saw the fall of the Paris fashion industry too. But much of their output went overseas – part of the huge export drive mentioned earlier. At home, fewer garments were available, even to those who could afford them. Berlei, the well-known makers of 'foundation garments', made a virtue of this in their advertising, hailing the fact that they were sending their products overseas as patriotic. They promised that 'any inconvenience or delay you may suffer now will be amply repaid when victory is achieved' – because, they said, the Berlei designers were busy creating brilliant designs, ready for the day when materials would be abundant again.

From 1941, clothes were rationed with a coupon or points system, just as food was: sixty-six coupons per year per person, reduced in 1942 to forty-eight, when even basics such as towels and tea towels were added to the list of rationed goods. Clothing retailers advertised wool coats at 'only two coupons a yard' and skirts became shorter and slimmer to save on material. The government introduced a 'utility' system, with the aim of economising on materials and labour and also of ensuring a certain level of quality.

Jean has preserved a memento of those days:

I still have a pillowcase with a utility mark on it – it was known as the 'two cheeses' but actually it was two capital Cs, short for 'Controlled Commodity'. Rationed clothing and linen and furniture all had this mark; it was the government's way of making scarce things go further. But this is the very pillowcase that I used to hang at the end of my bed on Christmas Eve. It's lasted quite well, hasn't it?

Many people saved up coupons to buy a Christmas treat; parents gave children clothes (which they needed anyway) as Christmas presents; and a barter system soon flourished between those who were short of clothes and those who were happy to swap clothing coupons for something else that they needed more.

Angela was a teenager during the war:

My father gave me his clothing coupons so that I could add them to mine and buy a coat. It was his Christmas present to me in 1943, when I was fourteen. I remember it so well: it was beige, a sort of corded material – not wool, but some substitute for wool. It had a high waist, just under the bust, and then it flared out from there, down to mid-calf length. It was my first grown-up coat and I just loved it, but I remember there being quite an upset at home because Dad had given me his coupons and Mum didn't think it was good for me to have everything I wanted.

She must have forgiven us, though, because by the next Christmas I was old enough to be allowed to go to dances at the local barracks and she made me a party dress out of parachute silk. It wasn't silk at all, it was more like nylon, but you could buy it in shops, as long as you had enough coupons. They even dyed it different colours and patterns. It was a lovely dress, made of two different materials. Tight under the bust and full from there down; a plain collar and plain skirt, but a floral pattern on the bodice and on panels set into the side of the skirt, so that there was a flash of flowery material when I danced. I remember being thrilled at having a dress like that for the barracks Christmas 'do'.

June also remembers parachute silk:

I became quite a good dressmaker, when I could get the material. Sometimes after a shop had been bombed and it was considered safe to go back in, they found undamaged stock in the cellar, and the government allowed this to be bought without coupons. And then there was parachute 'silk'. They'd obviously produced too much of it. A parachute was put together from a number of panels, and the shopkeepers would cut it up again, so you could buy a single panel or several panels – you didn't have to buy a whole parachute's worth! I remember one Christmas I made my mother a lovely petticoat out of parachute silk, as well as various pretty things for myself.

I also remember begging things from elderly relations – things they didn't wear any more, which I could turn into something for myself. I had been nine at the start of the war; when it ended I was fifteen; and by the time clothing came off the ration I was about eighteen. So the clothes I'd had at the start of the war were no good to me! I had a great-aunt who died in 1942 and when we were clearing out her house we found a whole trunk full of clothes – she'd obviously never thrown anything away. There was a tweed cloak that I made into a coat as a Christmas present for myself – it was good heavy tweed, very good quality, and it would have cost most of my coupons for six months if I'd bought it new.

But oh, I remember the day clothing came off the ration. It was several years after the war ended and we all went out and bought two pairs of shoes. Just because we could.

Jenny remembers a style that has mercifully fallen out of favour:

> There was a horrible fashion in those days for fox wraps that still had the fox's head, legs and tail on them. You might have a fur that went round your neck quite tightly, like a detached collar; or one that was flung over your shoulder like an old-fashioned pashmina. And there were short fur jackets and full-length coats – though they were more likely to be rabbit and didn't have the heads and tails. Really wealthy people had mink or sable. But during the war, when everything was in such short supply, furs came to be seen as a bit showy, a bit flash. My mother and my aunt put theirs away in the cellar, where it was cold, carefully wrapped up in cotton cloth, and only brought them out at Christmas. I remember my aunt rubbing her rabbit coat with sawdust soaked in something like white spirit, to clean it before she wore it to a party on Christmas Eve. You have to remember how cold many houses were in those days: whatever else they were, furs were certainly warm!

Country Life readers apparently didn't worry about being seen as showy. The magazine's Christmas issue of 1939 mentioned a shop in the City of London where one could buy furs as Christmas or New Year presents for very reasonable prices:

> Whether as an evening wrap or worn over a plain velvet or cloth suit, there would be something very out-of-

the-way and charming about the little cape with a hood in dyed Canadian squirrel which I saw the other day offered by the City Fur Store. A small jacket in chocolate brown Canadian ermine would have been even better for the woman who likes something uncommon but not too picturesque.

In 1940 its fashion feature was maintaining that 'nothing could take away from us the inner happiness of Christmas-time' and urging readers to reflect this in their homes with 'charming clothes that will do very much to brighten the scene on Christmas Day'. One of its recommendations was a 'really beautiful nutria coat, so soft and light and pliable, and yet so deliciously warm', which came with a 'darling little high fur cap with its gay knot of ribbon'. [Nutria was another name for the coypu, a rodent that was often farmed for its fur, but was a substantial step down the social scale from mink.]

In 1942 the magazine could still write about buying a new dress for oneself at Christmas, in 'thin wool or a thick crêpe marocain', but it noted the absence of trimming and of full pleated skirts. The skirt 'must be slim as a reed' and the dress's severity could be relieved by 'enormous chunky necklaces ... or row upon row of pearls'. The same article noted with approval that Elizabeth Arden had produced a white rabbit bolero – 'originally made as a bed jacket, but so smart and cosy that it is being bought for the house and for dinner to wear over black' – while the opposite page featured an advertisement for a full-length coat of 'natural racoon for hard wear'.

For those who didn't wear fur boleros over their black dinner dresses, 'make do and mend' was the order of the day. In 1941 *Good Housekeeping*'s Christmas edition gave the results of a competition to find the best children's clothes made from old adult garments. First prize went to a tailored little boy's coat made from a woman's coat that had been washed, unpicked and reversed, while runners-up included 'exquisite little smock and knickers made from a man's badly worn cotton shirt' and a siren suit for a little girl, 'made from an old coat, with lining made from an evening dress'.

Stockings were another luxury: once rationing began (and before the Americans introduced nylons), a lisle pair required two coupons, a silk pair three. Even before rationing, you did your best to make stockings last.

Sally, aged eighteen in 1940, and living in Manchester, remembers:

It was just before Christmas and what turned out to be the worst bombing raid of the entire war in Manchester. I was walking home from the cinema with my friend Thelma and two boys – we were dressed in our best because we wanted to impress these lads. Suddenly the air-raid warning went off and Thelma threw herself into a ditch. I was horrified. 'Get up,' I said, 'you'll ruin your stockings.' We were used to bombs by that time, but stockings were precious.

CHAPTER 5

'SPAM AND ALL THE TRIMMINGS'

Christmas has always been a time for family gatherings, and in the 1930s and 1940s many people still lived in close proximity to their parents, siblings and other relations, all of whom would converge on one of their houses for the festivities. War broke up many of these convivial gatherings and made others much more meagre. One of the most poignant things missing from many children's Christmases was their father. Sue, born in the first summer of the war, has photos of her father taken at her christening, but shortly after that, and with her younger sister 'on the way', he was sent to India and they didn't see him again for five years.

Rita in Northampton recalls:

I was about four when my dad went into the army; he was posted to Burma and I didn't see him again until the war was over, when I was about ten. Then of course there was the baby boom – I had started secondary school when my little brother was born.

Another little girl – aged two when her father left home and four when he fought in the Battle of El Alamein – wrote hoping that he was having a lovely time in Tripoli, not knowing that he would never return. Others sent drawings of themselves and the presents they had been given in their father's name.

Esme did her best to keep their father in the minds of her two small children:

From the time my son was three and my daughter a babe in arms, my husband never had leave at Christmas: that was three Christmases in a row that he wasn't home, and we didn't see much of him the rest of the time. He was a dentist with the Royal Army Dental Corps, stationed at Aldershot, so we knew he was safe, but it was difficult for tiny children to remember him from one visit to the next. One evening my son was asleep in the Morrison shelter in the living room and woke up to see a man in uniform standing in the doorway. He sat bolt upright, stretched out his arms in delight and cried, 'Daddy, Daddy!' But it wasn't his daddy – it was a young neighbour, home unexpectedly on leave, who had dropped by to see if his mother was with us. Bless him, he gave little Frankie a big hug, but I've never forgotten the look of disappointment on my son's face when the truth dawned on him.

Brenda, at seven, was old enough to be aware of her father's absence:

> Most of all, I remember the eagerly awaited parcel addressed to me personally, from Dad in London, with a wonderful book. I cannot emphasise enough what joy that brought me. I found it difficult to settle in at school in Aberdeen at first and I missed my father so much; therefore a book was more than a book to me – it was a friend! I don't recall Dad ever coming up north at that time of year – he wouldn't have had the long holidays we have now. Summer was his chosen time, when he could enjoy a game of golf.

Fathers missed their families, just as families missed them. Sentiments such as 'I dread Christmas, knowing I can't be with you all' and 'Perhaps this time next year it will all be over' occur again and again in letters home. Ellie's father, a doctor serving in the Middle East, worked hard to keep in touch with his children, especially at Christmas:

> Father sent gifts from Egypt, and they always arrived in good time, sewn into a linen bag of some sort – many of the troops did this, as it was more rip-proof than paper. His stitching was immaculate! It was like having him home with us, as he also wrote an airgraph – the letter that was photographed and sent as film to allow for more mail to be flown back to the UK from wherever the Forces were. He wrote six every week, apart from

the one time that he was in hospital as a patient: one to each of us (my mother and us four children), and on alternate weeks one to his mother and one to his mother-in-law.

For many people, even with Father at home, there was a lot to be sorrowful about. Diana was eight when war broke out:

We'd been a big family, so we were used to having a lovely time at Christmas, but during the war it was just my mum, my dad and me. Mum was bedridden and I had to look after her, so Christmas was very quiet with all my brothers away – it was just dull. I remember one year Dad killed our last chicken for dinner; but the next year we didn't have anything special. We didn't have enough rations to save for anything.

Dorothy in Chesterfield doesn't remember Christmas 1939 as a happy time:

The men were all away, of course, and Christmas celebrations were really for the little ones. My husband John was an engineer with the RAF, so I was living with my parents and we didn't do much. I knew John was safe, but it didn't seem right to celebrate with so many others suffering from anxiety or bereavement.

One very good friend, Roland, was a navigator in the RAF and was shot down on his first mission, in December 1939. The pilot insisted that Roland bale out, so he did – he later learned that the pilot had got safely back to France and landed his plane there. But Roland was taken prisoner and kept there for five years. His wife Virginia was supposed to be coming to us for Christmas – she lived in Derby, about thirty miles away – but of course she had just heard that he was missing. She rang me up and said, 'I don't think I will come' – she was so upset. We talked her into coming anyway, and when she arrived she was leaning out of the railway carriage window and waving: 'He's safe! He's safe!' After two days of complete anxiety, not knowing whether he was alive or dead, she'd heard from the Red Cross that he had been taken prisoner. It wasn't much cause for celebration, but it was a lot better than it might have been.

We had a training centre near us, with young lads who had just been recruited and were learning their jobs. There weren't nearly enough weapons for them, so they were drilling with rakes and hoes and things instead of rifles. My mother was a very kind woman and she took pity on them, being away from home for the first time. We tried hard to make it a normal family Christmas for them – and of course having young men around made it seem more normal for us, too.

Accounts of family gatherings are yet another indication of how conditions worsened as the war progressed. In 1939, the main difference from the previous year was the inconvenience of the blackout.

June, living in Andover, Hampshire, remembers:

Before the war, Woolworths used to have a lovely display at Christmas, and so did some of the smaller, privately owned stores. But the special feature of Andover was the Meat Show. Goodness knows what Health and Safety would think now, but the butchers used to hang their wares outside their shops, in the open air – not only sides of beef and pork, but chickens and pheasants, which were popular in our part of the world: a lot of people had pheasant for their Christmas dinner. So you could go up to the butcher and say, 'I'll take that one, please' or 'I'd like a cut of that' and choose your own meat. I was eight in 1938 and I think that was the first time my mother took me to see the Meat Show, because she thought I was old enough to appreciate it. By 1939 that was all gone – everything was blacked out, the shops shut earlier and after the war the displays never really recovered.

Rose was living in Bromley, Kent, and wrote detailed letters of family doings to her recently married sister in Zurich. In 1939, apart from the blackout, there was little to show that war had struck this well-to-do family:

Monday 11th December
Christmas shopping in the blackout is the most terrible business of all, especially when one does not know what to buy… We went first to a dress shop for Mum, but they did not have what we wanted, so we have put that off,

and she may get one later. By that time it was dark, of course, and of course the crowds in the High Street are awful, and one keeps bumping into people and falling off the pavement, and getting tied up with dogs, and in the drizzle of course some people had umbrellas up and they were death traps. I did not buy a single thing for presents, only a veil to refurbish up my old hat. Mum did not buy anything either except the usual weekend shopping. It is impossible to look in shop windows once the blackout starts, and unless one goes in Woolworths, Boots or Medhursts [department store] *and looks round, there is no hope of getting anything. We arrived back about 6.30 with not much to show for our pains.*

Christmas Day

We decided we would try to have dinner about 5, so as to give us a longer evening. After breakfast we put up the dining room blackout, as it was fairly dark anyway, then we did the usual tidying up in all the rooms and got all the fires going, and then Dad took Bob [the family's dog] *for his pub-crawl. Mum gave him instructions to get back at 2.30 for our drink with you. Oh I am leaving out the most important part. After breakfast, we all gathered round the fire, and Dad turned out his pillow case, and I made a tidy pile of all the string and paper. Dad had his usual pile, of course, cigars, tobacco, cigarettes, bath salts etc. Then we all gave out our presents. By the time everyone had brought in their presents ready to give out, the dining room looked like the General Post Office, and it was difficult to move. You know what big boxes and parcels we have usually. I set the ball rolling, and we spent another hour or more giving and receiving parcels. I will try and remember what I had. For fillups there were:– brown suede gas mask carrier, stockings, navy skirt and navy jumper, navy wool for a cardigan, a three in one clip, two lots of bath salts, sweeties, panties, bath cubes, hankies from Chris.*

For presents an umbrella from May, lovely pair of gloves from Lil and Albert and also stockings from Albert. Sylvia gave Lil and I a big box of chocs. I also had a toilet case with face cloth and towel from Snook, and scent from Miss Harcourt.

Well, at about 2.15 we went into the drawing room to listen to the Empire broadcast. I wonder if you listened. I expect you did. This year of course it was a little different, first the R.A.F., then France, and the Navy. We got ready the glasses and drink first and at about 2.25 Dad came in and we had our drinks on time. I hope you did too. Mum of course was popping in and out seeing to the turkey and listening to the programme. Then of course the King came on, and I got quite tensed up when he had such difficulty at first in speaking. However, he got better, don't you think, in the middle. I expect that broadcast spoilt his whole morning, I expect he was a bundle of nerves, but anyway it was a very good broadcast and the reception all over the empire was very good. I hope Hitty listened in. I expect he did on the quiet, although he was 'with his troops on the Western Front'.

During the afternoon we had some more tea and a

mince pie or pork sandwich or so just to keep us going, and then went up to dress. I wore my bridesmaid's frock as Albert and Sylvia had not seen it, Albert was in tails, Dad in uniform, Chris in Dinner jacket, Lil in her black and white, Mum in blue velvet, etc., etc. We managed to get dinner at 5.30 which was not so bad, what. Of course the turkey was voted the best we ever had, also the ham, which just melted. Brussels, parsnips, baked potatoes, etc., all went the same way home and everyone chewed away. Mum got a 15 lb turkey this year instead of the 20 lb, as of course there are only the three of us to finish up the remains, and we should be a long time at it. Anyway it was the usual lovely bird. Christmas pud and custard were the same as usual. For wines, we did not have champagne this year, but had Graves which was very nice indeed, then port, then Curacoa for liqueur with our coffee. I like Curacoa the best, I think, it is very nice and smooth and not sharp like some. Then everybody seemed to tuck into nuts, as though they had had nothing to eat, and mince pies. Then we adjourned to the drawing room, and squeezed ourselves round the fire as usual, and listened to the wireless by the light of the fire, and half snoozed the way we usually do.

A year later, the tone was very different:

Mum had been promised sausages with her turkey, but apparently there was none available, only sausage meat, so Dad had brought that home, and of course Mum

129

*was very peeved. She said everything went wrong on
Christmas Eve. A woman in the shop told Dad to roll the
sausage meat in flour and fry it and it would be just the
same, so of course Mum had to do that. It tasted all right,
but of course looked a bit funny and all knobbly....*

*The turkey was very nice and also all my own
vegetables, Brussels, parsnips, potatoes. May had bread
sauce with hers, but we did not. It was very funny to see
Albert carving the ham. You know he always does while
Dad does the turkey. Well, hams are unobtainable now,
as we know them, but during the summer Mum had
got a little tin of ham, and warmed it up, so there was
Albert with a nice big dish, and that great big ham knife,
trying to slice ham 4 inches square. It was very funny.
Afterwards we had the Christmas pud, and it was as
black as the blackout, but had cooked too long, so it all
fell to pieces. Then we sat round the dining room fire for
a bit and had a drop of coffee, but Lil and Sylvia made
it and either it hadn't drawn or they had not put enough
coffee in or something, but it was extremely weak. We
were not dressed up at all, and had not lit the fire in the
drawing room. Can you imagine that?*

In 1941 the family again failed to get into what Rose referred
to as their 'glad rags'. There was no description of dinner and
the presents had taken a more practical turn:

*I had a pair of slippers from Albert and Sylvia, from
May I had a book, 'Europe to Let' which looks quite*

*interesting, a pair of slippers she made, and some bath
salts. From Lil some Saving Certificates stamps, from
Mum some Saving Certificates stamps and some cash. I
seem to have bought most of my Christmas presents just
in time this year (I have been collecting them all the year
anyway), the hot water bottles I bought for Christmas
are now going to be unobtainable (they were just before
Christmas, a week after I bought them). I bought Dad a
boiler suit for grubbing about in, and now one has to give
up coupons, I bought Mum an eiderdown in August, and
they are in short supply, so I seem to have been a bit lucky
in my purchases.*

Joan, from Suffolk, a small child during the war, remembers
her family gatherings as happy ones:

We always had a Christmas tree that Dad collected
from the woods. We'd clip real candles on it – little red
twisted ones, about the size of your finger. We'd light
them only for a few minutes and watch them closely in
case of fire.

Most families had a 'best room', as we did, so there
was big excitement when a fire was lit, decorations put
up, Christmas tree in the corner, ready for a family party
– Nana, Granddad and friends all came for Christmas
tea. We'd sing carols and songs – Granddad's favourite
was 'Jolly Jack the Sailor Boy', maybe because he had
been a sailor in his younger days. I can't remember ever
being short of food – maybe because we lived on a farm

and had a good supply of milk and eggs, the odd rabbit or pheasant, and of course plenty of fruit and veg.

My mum used to swap her clothing coupons, giving them to a well-off lady, in return for food: large tins of apricot jam and rough brown sugar. I suppose this was what they called the black market, but it all helped to make Christmas better. We always had a Christmas stocking – one of Mum's old lisle stockings – with an orange wrapped in tissue paper in the toe. We had to save this paper for the lavatory – it was better than the newspaper squares neatly hung on a nail in our bucket toilet up the garden.

Wendy, living in fairly comfortable circumstances in Surrey, was six when war broke out. She was the third of four children:

Because we lived in a safe and rural area, lots of the horror passed us by, and the Christmases only seem unusual by comparison. We were so used to blackout, cold houses and food rationing that they were taken for granted. I do remember Christmas decorations, and the annual making of paper chains was something the four of us really enjoyed. They were bought in small packets and when made up were frequently kept for next year. We did have a string of fairy lights, which my father spent hours repairing every year, and I think the tree was dug up from the garden.

We children often made presents for our parents. A painting with a tiny calendar bought from Woolworth, with a twisted silk loop added at the top to hang it up. I once bought a handkerchief for my mother for sixpence three farthings – less than 3p.

Christmas pudding was an annual event. As kids we skinned the almonds and stoned the raisins. There was a ritual to stir the pud and make a wish; my father did this before he went to work the day of the cooking, some weeks before Christmas Day itself. We always had Christmas stockings, though no oranges or sweets or chocolate. Nevertheless it was exciting – a balloon was an exotic feature to be blown up and a tragedy if it burst because you only got one. Pencils and rubbers always featured, maybe a painting book and once a torch. We stayed awake till Father Christmas had delivered, then lay awake for an age listening for the parents to go to bed. A quick feel in the dark to see what he had brought, then sleep till 6 a.m. or so. But we had bigger presents too, later on Christmas morning: the most treasured ones I remember from my parents were a fountain pen and a wrist watch.

I remember saving wrapping paper and string for years. My mother was a great storer of everything, from tinned, home-bottled and pickled food to string, brown paper, newspapers and even worn-out cotton underwear, which was used for cleaning and polishing. At Christmas, the same old pieces of holly paper and ragged string were used over and over.

I also remember it was always very cold. One year my grandparents came to stay and whatever car they were travelling in got stuck in snow at the bottom of the hill: I have no memories of the resolution.

We kept chickens and rabbits in the back garden, and ate one of the chickens for Christmas dinner. I don't remember noticing that we went short of anything, even drink for my parents, who were mainly gin and whisky drinkers. I don't know where supplies came from, but my grandfather wasn't above dabbling in the black market. I am sure they always had champagne and claret at Christmas, which he probably had from a pre-war stock. I remember he once produced a Château d'Yquem, which must have been expensive, but my parents preferred hock and had beautiful hock glasses with barley-sugar stems. Grandpa was no doubt the provider.

Joan, living in Cardiff and the eldest of four children, also had quite a privileged time:

My father was a policeman, which was a well-paid job, and we never went without. We kept two pigs, chickens and about forty rabbits, so there was never any shortage of meat, and there were plenty of vegetables from Dad's garden. The only things I remember being short of were butter and sugar. We weren't rich, but we were certainly comfortable: all four of us children went to the grammar school, which was practically unheard of in those days, and we were one of only two families in our street who owned a car.

My father was born in Dowlais, near Merthyr Tydfil in the Welsh Valleys, but had moved to Cardiff for his work. That meant that we had quite quiet Christmases

– just the six of us, because my grandparents were up in the Valleys and with the petrol rationing we couldn't go to visit them, nor bring them to us.

A lot of our presents were second-hand, but my father was a marvellous handyman and he could refurbish anything, so that you'd never know it wasn't new. I had two sisters and then a brother, and I remember we three girls being given things like a doll's house and a doll's pram, to be shared between us. Presents like games would be given to one of us, but with a label saying 'To be shared with the family', and we would all play with them together.

One thing we were never short of at Christmas was sweets or chocolate. We used to save up all our rations and go with my mother to the sweet shop, where they had sweets loose in those big jars that sweet shops used to have. Anyway, we were allowed to put our hands in the different jars and choose what we wanted. Then they would be hidden away and not opened until Christmas morning.

Well, both my sisters used to get through all their sweets by Boxing Day – and I'm talking about perhaps two pounds in weight of sweets each. I used to make mine last, but for days or weeks afterwards my sisters would complain about how mean I was, because I refused to share my sweets with them. My mother always backed me up: 'You all had the same rations,' she'd say. 'You all chose what you wanted. It's not Joan's fault if you've eaten all of yours.'

Biddy's father was the rector of a parish in Rutland, so Christmas celebrations took second place to his duties:

The rectory was an enormous Jacobean building, said to be haunted, and it had a large Victorian walled garden. We grew lots of vegetables – I'm sure we never went hungry – and we kept geese and always had goose for Christmas dinner. There'd often be quite a crowd of us: I had two sisters a lot older than myself, but my parents used to take in other children whose parents were overseas – some of them were our cousins, some weren't related at all, but there are photos of lots of children, perhaps eight or ten of us, lined up in order of age.

Father had to conduct the morning service, then we'd have our meal and open presents before the King's Speech. The king had a terrible stutter and it was agony listening to him. He'd get so far, then stumble and there'd be a long pause as we waited for him to get the next words out. I used to imagine the whole country waiting with bated breath, praying for him to get through it.

There was a big Air Force camp nearby and Australian and New Zealand airmen used to come in for tea – poor souls, they would end up being dragged away to play ping-pong with me. One of my sisters married a New Zealander and all through the war his mother sent us a lovely Christmas cake, because she thought everyone in England was very short of food. Years later I visited New Zealand and learned that they had been short of food, too; it was only then that I realised just what a kind gesture this had been.

Not all family gatherings went smoothly, as Marjorie remembers:

I had a stepfather and he was a glutton for food – a bit of a brute, really – so an awful lot of our rations went to him. I remember after our meal one night – it must have been a few weeks before Christmas – he said to my mum, 'Is that all we've got?' And all of a sudden, she went into the kitchen and came out with a few crackers and the Christmas cake. 'It's not Christmas,' he said. 'What are you doing?' But she was so annoyed, she plunked it down in front of him and said, 'Here you are. Eat the bloody lot!' And I remember being horrified that we weren't going have any Christmas cake for Christmas.

My mother had managed to get a goose from somewhere, and she'd invited my aunt and cousin over for Christmas, because we had plenty to go round. They came in the evening on Christmas Eve and the goose was in the oven – it was going to cook slowly overnight. Everyone was sitting in the living room and after a couple of hours my mother went into the kitchen to check how the goose was doing. And she went flying. The roasting tin had a little slit in it and the goose fat was all over the kitchen floor. And there's a lot of fat in a goose! So at eleven o'clock on Christmas Eve night, my poor mother and Auntie Jean were down on their knees with floor cloths, cleaning the kitchen floor.

Sue in Sussex also has memories of a goose causing havoc at Christmas:

My mother had three little girls under three years old. I don't remember much about that time, of course, but there are lots of stories that my mother used to tell. At first we had servants, including a nanny; later there was just a series of girls who came in to look after us. Mum had a big 'sit up and beg' bicycle with a seat on the back, so my elder sister rode in that as soon as she was old enough; and we had one of those old-fashioned prams with enormous wheels. You could take something out of the middle of it to fit two babies in, one facing forwards and the other facing back, so Diana and I rode in that whenever we went up the hill to my grandmother's, which we did every Sunday and on Christmas Day. The nanny or maid must have come with us, I suppose, because Mum couldn't have pushed the pram while she was riding her bike, but I don't remember for sure. But I do know that as soon as we could walk, we were taken out for walks: by the last Christmas of the war – when I was four – I would have been walking the quarter-mile or so uphill to my grandmother's house.

We were living in an old and very, very cold sort of Elizabethan barn that had been converted into a house.

The people we rented it from had had an air-raid shelter built in the garden: from the outside it just looked like a mound under the oak tree. We never went in there for protection, but it was a wonderful hidey-hole and home for the local wildlife. We used to go in there to find frogs.

My grandmother's was much warmer – a lovely old village house. She had a big, big table and we would all sit round it: my mother, the three of us, my grandmother, her sister and various other relations – cousins of some sort – plus a cousin of my father's who was probably just finishing school at that time, but who seemed quite grown up to us.

Christmas would be always goose; turkeys really hadn't hit the market in the way that they did after the war. My grandmother kept geese – Chinese geese, the big white ones with a funny knob on their bill – but it wasn't a Chinese goose that we ate; she bought a live one from somewhere. And there was one amazing occasion – I don't remember this at all, but I was told about it many times – when the goose had had its neck wrung and had been plucked, ready to be drawn and put into the oven next day. There was no fridge, so it was put in the cellar to keep cool overnight. The next morning it was found to be alive and kicking but, of course, featherless. It couldn't possibly be cooked, so that Christmas we didn't have goose, we had chicken. And this goose was knitted a jersey to keep it warm until its feathers grew again. It never was disposed of

– it was always there in my grandmother's garden, this big white goose, until long after the war.

We had fresh vegetables from the garden. Boiled or steamed potatoes – I don't think we roasted them. Brussels sprouts and whatever else was ready for Christmas time. A traditional Christmas lunch. It wasn't possible to get much dried fruit, though, so we didn't have a traditional Christmas pudding. We would have something made from stored fruit, from some autumn gathering or other – apple pie or something like that, with custard made from powdered egg. But we were always well-fed at my grandmother's; I don't remember ever not having a good meal there.

Pauline is another who, as a small child, had to walk to her grandparents, for a big family Christmas:

It was about two miles, and I don't know if we always had white Christmases in those days, but I remember trudging along through the snow. My grandmother used to set the table in the back room – we used to have two sittings, because not everybody could get round the table at once, but if you were on the second sitting there wasn't much left!

Mollie, aged about eight, recalls what could have been a traumatic experience:

At some point during the war my brother, who was

older than me, cottoned on to the idea that Father Christmas didn't exist. I didn't want to believe him, so he was determined to keep me awake so that I could see for myself. He kept nudging me and saying, 'Are you awake? Are you awake?' Eventually, of course, we both fell asleep. So although we had our doubts, we couldn't prove that Father Christmas was really Dad.

A year or two later, she *did* have a trauma:

Like many people, I used to have a stone hot water bottle – the rubber ones were hard to come by and expensive during the war. You put boiling water in and it stood upright in the bed and radiated heat to warm your feet (I only remember getting one chilblain – other people had them forever). Our house was freezing cold. It was semi-detached, much colder than the terraced one where my friend lived warmly.

One Christmas morning I emptied the water from my hot-water bottle into the bowl in the bathroom. It slipped out of my hand and smashed the bowl. Even my father realised it was an accident, but I do remember the atmosphere was tense because everything shut down over Christmas, so there was no way of getting it repaired. And the expense!

Christine was part of a big family whose aunt, uncle and cousin lived next door:

My father had a lot of brothers and sisters and they all used to come to us for Christmas. During the war we moved up North for a couple of years, but were back on the outskirts of London in 1944 and revived the traditional family Christmas. My father and his brothers were all too old to be called up – they were ARP Wardens and in the Home Guard and that sort of thing, but none of them were away in the Forces. The men stayed at our place and the women and children slept next door. That's because there were five children in our family and Auntie Alice had only one daughter, so she had more room.

My mother and Auntie Alice would share their coupons so that they could buy larger quantities of food, and the women would all bring something to contribute to the meal. The rule was that the men looked after the children while the women were doing the cooking. I was twelve and too old to need looking after, but I remember a lot of noise and hilarity and one of the baubles on the Christmas tree being broken. My mother was furious because they'd been saved up from before the war and you couldn't buy replacements. Nobody else seemed to care – I don't think any of the fathers were as strict as our mothers, and I've always suspected that the culprit was Uncle Mike, rather than any of the children. He was the youngest and tended to be a bit boisterous.

Celebrations lasted no more than twenty-four hours. Everyone would arrive on Christmas morning, stay one night and go home straight after lunch on Boxing Day. After that it was back to work as if nothing had happened.

Marion from Glasgow remembers that in Scotland, Christmas Day was quite an ordinary day:

My dad was a cabinet-maker and he went to work on Christmas Day; he came home at lunchtime and we had just the normal lunch – soup and tatties and mince or stew. But we had hung up our stockings on Christmas Eve and in the morning found them filled with a threepenny bit, an orange and other little things like that. My parents were great readers, so we always got a book at Christmas and one other present, which might be a new doll or new knitted clothes for an old doll.

The first Sunday after Christmas Day was our big celebration: we went to my Auntie Maggie's for a 'party'. There was Mum and Dad and the three of us; another aunt and uncle and their three children; and Auntie Maggie and her husband, Uncle Dougie. Auntie Maggie didn't have any children and she saved all her coupons for months so she could give this party. We didn't have turkey, but tongue, and always what we Scots call a 'dumpling' – a pudding full of dried fruit and spices, steamed in a cloth – with silver sixpences in it. As presents, Auntie May knitted jumpers for us and gave us sweets. Then for tea we had cakes and tinned fruit.

In the afternoon we played games and cards and left for home about 9 p.m., having had a lovely time.

Another Scot adds:

My parents didn't normally have drink in the house, but they always had a bottle of whisky and a bottle of sherry at Hogmanay. They'd have a very good party, but then that would be it until the following year.

Ellie, aged ten when war broke out and living in Aberdeen, did better than most:

We were fortunate in being a doctor's house. Mother (who ran the practice while Father was in the Middle East) got extra coal and petrol. We could change our sweetie ration into sugar, so my brother and I lost our sweets, much to our disgust. But the sugar was used to make jam with the fruit that was plentiful in our large garden. We were also allowed to have a live-in cook/housekeeper, whereas other families lost their staff – they were called up to the services or to munitions factories.

Many of the patients were shopkeepers and at Christmas Mother received gifts of dried fruit to make a cake and Christmas pudding, and she was able to buy two turkeys, one for us and one for my granny, my father's mother who lived very near us. We had Christmas dinner at home and New Year's Day across at Granny's house. She was a real trooper, and had my other grandmother in from Insch, about thirty miles away, for the week, so that she could share the festivities. So our Christmas was luckier than that of many other people.

Anyway, Christmas preparations went on as usual, and the present-opening was fairly normal. Books were the favourite gift, which suited all of us, as we read voraciously. Aggie, the cook, got presents from all of us, mostly toiletries, as toothpaste and talc weren't rationed. We saved the wrapping paper and ironed it for use next year!

One thing we weren't short of in Aberdeen was fish. In the days before the NHS was formed, the patients were billed, and many of them paid in kind. The North Sea fishermen paid in fish, and the farmers paid in rabbits and cream, which was a great help at Christmas. But in London fish was as scarce as hen's teeth. My granny had a brother who was a minister there, and she used to buy fish every week and put it on the overnight train to King's Cross, where Uncle Josie would retrieve it the next morning.

I can't remember any big disappointments at Christmas, although I suppose there must have been a few. Always in the stocking there were a few titbits, such as nuts, mandarins, an apple and a sweetie or two. We just got used to going without some things, and we always knew we were better off than most.

Jean's experience was rather different, as her father was in the Royal Indian Army:

For my family, Christmas would be spent wherever my father happened to be stationed that year. My mother usually spent the summer months in the Himalayan hills at Simla (now called Shimla), where I and my cousins were boarders at a school run on very English lines. School term ended in the middle of December, when the school disbanded and we all climbed aboard the narrow-gauge railway to travel to the foothill station of Kalkha. Then we split up and went in all directions to our parents.

Christmas preparations followed the usual pattern – a letter to Father Christmas listing hoped-for items (I got my bike, hooray) and making the pudding, not forgetting to include the tiny silver trinkets which would be duly admired and then solemnly returned to be stored for next year. Our Christmas stockings held some fruit in the toe – nuts and small gifts – while the bigger things would be lurking under the tree.

We didn't do much shopping, and being in a military environment my mother was involved in some 'war work', with which we girls were expected to join, cutting out and rolling bandages, knitting interminably long scarves in air-force blue. One year there was a convoy of troops expected on their way east, and a vast quantity of Christmas pudding ingredients was amassed for my mother to take part in a marathon steaming session.

On Christmas Day we attended church before lunch, and were bidden to think about the families who had lost members amid the terrible carnage in Europe. My own grandmother steadfastly remained in Sussex throughout the war.

The Indian cook was completely in charge of the food, and the servants all had their share of presents and joined in the fun afterwards – including, sometimes, cricket on the lawn. They were really our extended family.

Christmas was also a time when a lot of people got married. With the prospect of death always just around the corner, there was a sense of urgency; during the early part of the war, at least, it was also a time when people might be lucky enough to have leave and families could get together.

For Helen's family, this began a series of tragic events:

My parents were married on Boxing Day 1939. They'd brought the wedding forward because it was the only day that everyone could get the day off. In November 1940 they were in Southampton and they had a direct hit on the house. My grandparents were killed, my uncle was killed, another uncle was blown – in his bed – out on to Southampton Common. My mother lost the baby she was expecting and woke up in a padded cell in a psychiatric hospital because there was a shortage of beds. Nobody told her this was the reason – she was terrified, thinking she must have gone mad. My father had to have an operation on his back and on that very day he had a letter from the government telling him he was a deserter...

They had nothing left but life itself. Neither of them knew the other had survived. They were reunited on Boxing Day, their first wedding anniversary. They had no home – they had to move in with my cousins. It's a miracle that my sister and I were ever born and that we are alive today.

Carol's memories are happier:

I was married at Christmas 1941: we knew in advance that my fiancé was going to get leave, so we decided to do it while we could. He was home for forty-eight hours and then sent back to his station – that was all the honeymoon we had.

I had a beautiful long white dress, with lace and a Medici collar and a train and a veil – a great extravagance; it took all my points, and my mother's and my grandmother's. Over the next few years I lent it to four friends who got married while rationing was still in place and then years later I donated it to the local amateur dramatics company. So it had a long and useful life.

Ben also did his bit of recycling:

Christmas Day 1942 was a Friday, so Monday 28th

was a holiday, the official Boxing Day. That's the day we got married, because I was due back in Portsmouth on the Tuesday and my dad, who had a little grocery shop, refused to close on a Saturday. I gave my bride my great-aunt's wedding ring, not as a romantic gesture but because there was a shortage of them, too. In fact there was a bit of a scandal about that in the papers – how could people get married decently if there weren't any wedding rings? – so the Board of Trade increased production. If we'd waited six months to be married, Lily might have had a new ring! But we stayed married for sixty-one years, so she can't have minded too much.

Many a family wouldn't have been complete without its pets, although a tragically large number of these had been put to sleep in the early part of 1939. There had been a widespread belief that the war would begin with a massive campaign of air raids and poison-gas attacks, injuring many animals and leaving others homeless. The government was also concerned that when food shortages bit, pet owners would either share their rations with their pets or be forced to leave the animals to starve. The National Air Raid Precautions Animals Committee was formed to advise pet owners on what to do and the official line was, 'If you cannot place them in the care of neighbours, it really is kindest to have them destroyed.'

Animal lovers swung into action. Owners of kennels and catteries in safe rural areas offered happy, quiet accommodation for city pets; wealthy activists opened their country homes to animal refugees; hundreds of thousands of pet owners from the vulnerable cities and ports took their pets with them to welcoming boarding houses or sent them to stay with country-based relatives (where urban dogs unfamiliar with rural etiquette frequently made themselves unpopular by worrying sheep). Talk of providing dogs and cats with gas masks or finding ways of accommodating pets in gas-proof rooms filled the hobbyist press. But despite all these precautions, some 750,000 pets were destroyed before and immediately after the declaration of war.

Further problems arose once rationing began. Cats had to succumb to the indignity of having their milk watered down: two pints per adult per week didn't leave much to spare for the cat. The manufacturers of Chappie dog food issued an advertisement advising dog owners to apologise to their pets for the shortage of food and to suggest that they 'bark for the downfall of Hitler'. The same ad recommended that bones – even 'ones your dog has done with' – should be salvaged and put out for collection. In an era when nothing was allowed to go to waste, bones could be made into fertiliser or glue and used in the manufacture of explosives.

Nevertheless, people kept their pets: not only cats and dogs, but budgies, rabbits and chickens. More than one person has reminisced that their dog sensed the approach of bombers before the air-raid warnings went off, and began to herd its family towards the safety of the shelters. Others took their dogs out 'spotting doodlebugs': one member of the Home Guard recalled that his dog's keen hearing picked up the approaching flying bombs, and he was able to issue warnings more quickly than he would have done had he been patrolling on his own. And one remembered that, as a small girl, when the sirens sounded she used to hide under the dining room table with the cat.

As for Christmas, in 1940 the charity Our Dumb Friends League (later to become Blue Cross) gave a party in their headquarters in London for dogs that had been bombed out of their homes. The church cat of St Magnus the Martyr near London Bridge gave birth in the manger that was part of the church's festive display. A small boy visiting the church is said to have exclaimed, 'Baby kittens with mother Jesus!' And a cat lover writing to *The Cat* magazine reported having seen 'a huge black Tom curled up very cosily upon the straw within the manger. He was not the official church cat, but may have been invited in by the resident puss – one never knows.'

Dogs were fed on anything that was going, as George recalls: 'My mum would cook extra potatoes, and there were always vegetables being cooked to feed the chickens, so the dogs got bits of that.'

Nora's family managed to keep their dog in London:

I suppose we fed it any scraps that we might have had. We had a neighbour who kept chickens and we used to exchange: we'd give her things like cabbage leaves to feed the hens, and she'd give us the odd bone to feed the dog.

Tony's family pet found his own way round the rationing problem:

My mother's sister married a local butcher, so we never went short of meat during the war. One Christmas Eve morning my uncle drove over in his van and gave us a lovely leg of pork. In those days, we didn't have a fridge – we just had a little box on the outside of the house, with a mesh over it, where we used to keep milk and bacon and stuff like that. So perhaps it wasn't big enough for this leg of pork. Anyway, the pork went into the oven for safekeeping and my mum decided – what with all the extra things she was going to have to do on Christmas Day – that she'd cook it that afternoon, Christmas Eve, and serve it cold with gravy the next day.

We normally had our evening meal about six, but Dad always got a bit peckish later on, and that night he said, 'I could just fancy some of that pork.'

'Well, go and make yourself a sandwich,' Mum said. 'There's plenty.' So he did.

We had an Alsatian at the time, Micky was his name, and he was in the kitchen. Dad made his sandwich, put the pork back into the oven and came back into the front room, where were we listening to the radio. Later, when it was time to take Micky out, Dad found that he hadn't actually closed the oven door. So Micky had got in there, got the pork out and there was nothing left but the bone. We couldn't get Micky off the floor – we had to lift him up, he was so heavy with all this meat.

We didn't have a telephone or a car, and my uncle and aunt lived three miles away; there was no way we could get in touch with them at that hour. So Mum did whatever she could. She had some corned beef, there was a tin of Spam – and that's what we had to have. And the worst of it was that my aunt and my uncle the butcher were coming to Christmas lunch with us, so they had to have Spam with stuffing and all the trimmings too!

Cats and dogs continued to be treated as pets, but woe betide those who became too fond of their rabbits. Monica, aged five in 1940 and living in the East End of London, believed for many years that hers had escaped during an air raid:

My mother told me some complicated story about an incendiary bomb burning the lock off their hutch, and assured me that they would be safe in a burrow on Hackney Downs. I must have been impressed by the detail she went into, because I never questioned it. It wasn't until years after the war, when my mother was dead, that an aunt confessed to me that we had eaten the rabbits for Christmas dinner. We were often hungry in those days, so I suppose my mother was desperate. Looking back, I'm just glad we didn't have a cat or a dog.

Mary, born in 1939, had a similar experience. Many years later she was asked to give a talk at her children's primary school about what life had been like during the war:

I told them that we had kept rabbits in the back garden, and after my talk some of the children went sobbing back to their teacher and said, 'Mary used to eat her tame rabbits!' I had to explain that it wasn't really like that. We hadn't kept the rabbits as pets – I remember quite clearly that my mother discouraged us from giving them names – and we wouldn't necessarily recognise individuals: they were just there, playing around in their hutch in the backyard. We were sometimes told that one or two of them had gone to Granny's for a holiday, and I certainly never associated that with what turned up on our plates on Christmas Day.

CHAPTER 6

'A DAB HAND AT FLOUR-AND-WATER PASTE'

Like most other non-essentials, Christmas decorations virtually disappeared from the shops once the war started. Then as now, people stored them away from year to year, or made their own.

Colin remembers a family tradition that he thinks was passed down from his Norwegian grandmother:

Even during the war you could buy sheets of coloured paper, and we used these to make baskets to hang on the tree. We'd cut out two elongated semicircles, in different colours, each about eight inches long. Then we'd cut from the straight end almost to the top, so that each semicircle had three long, flapping legs. Finally, we'd weave the legs together and glue another strip of paper on top. It was slow and fiddly, but if we did it right the baskets were strong enough to hold sweets. Not that there were many sweets around, but my grandmother used to magic up a few at Christmas time.

Less demanding were the ubiquitous paper chains, made and hung in almost every household, school and church hall. Ros also remembers buying coloured paper:

They came in strips, in different colours, pinks, blues, yellows, greens. You'd glue them into circles, link them together to make chains, and drape them across the room. We did it at home and we used to do it at school too. We had a tree, a real tree – I don't know where it came from – and we used these chains to decorate that as well. I remember my mother and me sitting for hours with a brush and a pot of white glue – Gloy, it was called – making these strips into circles and then into chains, so that we had enough to go all over the room. But at school we didn't even have glue: we made a paste out of flour and water. There was no tinsel or anything shiny like that – it was just coloured paper. I remember quite clearly the first time we had the sort of fancy baubles you have nowadays, because I'd just got engaged and my fiancé was with us. So I was twenty and that was a good bit after the war.

Albert's father was a stationmaster and in 1944 the family moved to Garstang in Lancashire, where he was in charge of Garstang and Catterall, an important interchange between the local railway and the major London and North Western line:

> There was a paper mill nearby, in the village of Oakenclough. I think it was Jackson's. Among the things they produced were Christmas decorations and Dad somehow used to receive these – boxes and boxes of them – at Christmas. Almost everything went by railway then – you didn't have the road transport – so Jackson's did their 'shipping' via Dad's railway, and I think they paid him in kind: they gave him decorations as part of the fee for moving their goods.
>
> Anyway, there were the strips of paper that we made into paper chains, and there were the decorations made out of tissue paper, with cardboard in the centre and you clipped them at the back and made them into a bell. During the rest of the year we had nothing in the house – no decorations whatsoever – but coming up for Christmas you couldn't move for these things. The rooms were absolutely festooned with them, from the corners to the lampshade in the centre of the room. I was six in 1944 and having decorations all over the place was very exciting: we'd certainly never had anything like it before.

At the Foundling Hospital Schools in Berkhamsted, Lorna rather wistfully remembers a splendid tree:

> At Christmas, they moved two of the long tables, pushed them up closer together, and there was a massive

beautiful Christmas tree. That tree was so beautifully decorated that it had toys on it. I mean open toys like a teddy bear or a rabbit, not in boxes, but open for you to see. It was beautifully done with baubles and things and we used to sing carols and dance around the tree, once or twice when we were allowed to do so. But every year of course those toys and baubles et cetera went back in boxes for the next year.

Crackers were one thing that couldn't be used from year to year, so Pauline remembers making her own:

We'd cut out strips of cardboard and roll them up, then cover them in crepe paper of various colours. We'd twist the ends of the paper and tie bows and tinsel round them. We didn't have anything to put in them, and nothing to make them 'crack', but they looked pretty on the table.

Roy in Ealing made crackers in rougher surroundings:

I do recall that with the other two youngsters in the cellar, we made some 'bon-bons' as they were called [crackers] with odd bits of coloured paper around a cardboard tube. Handwritten silly jokes were inserted, together with any odd small items we could find.

No 'crack' strips. Anything that went bang was put to a more practical use! When pulled, we just shouted, 'BANG!' We were easily pleased in those days.

A soldier makes
the most of his last
moments at home.

Above: Boys at a Dr Barnardo's home make merry in an air-raid shelter they decorated themselves at Christmas, 1940.

Right: Westminster Council offered a prize for the best dressed shelter. This contender embellishes traditional decorations with flags and portraits of the King and Queen and Winston Churchill.

Father Christmas causes a stir as he hands out presents to evacuees from
Peckham, 1940.

Above: An Anderson shelter in Ilford is festively decorated for one sleepy child to wake up to on Christmas morning.

Right: Mistletoe and gas masks: a comic photo posed by Londoners to demonstrate how air-raid warnings could dampen the romantic spirit at Christmas.

Above: A group of children lug home sprigs of holly for decoration.

Below: German soldiers celebrate Christmas in a dugout on the Western Front, December 1939.

Above: Father Christmas swaps his sleigh for a tank, arriving at a party thrown by the US Army engineer stations for British war orphans.

Below left: Children standing on sandbags peer into the warm glow of a West End toy shop at Christmas, 1939.

Below right: A tiny tot clutches a haul of goodies and a miniature Christmas tree.

Above: During a broadcast from America by the British-American Ambulance Corps 'Friendship Bridge', three sisters evacuated from England sing to their parents over the radio.

Below: The last supper: Land Girls on an Essex farm round up the last of their turkeys.

Above: Two Royal Navy sailors carry Christmas trees and holly from a destroyer at Liverpool's Gladstone Dock two days before Christmas.

Below: War or no war, Santa Claus is always sure to come to town.

Christmas cards were not sent through the post and were not being made anyway. This would constitute a waste of valuable time and paper. However, the newsagents along the road found a couple of pre-war packs, and for a laugh we gave one to each of our regular shelter guests, captioned 'Thank you for sleeping with us.'

For Tony's family, decorating for Christmas was a great excitement:

We always had a Christmas tree; people with kids generally did. We bought them from the greengrocer; they weren't very expensive. Sometimes we'd get one with a root on and try to plant it in the garden afterwards, but it was never very successful. More often they were sold as they are today, stuck in a bit of tree trunk to hold them up. Three days after Christmas everywhere was covered in needles and it was my job to clear up the mess. We normally used a carpet sweeper to clean the floor, but it wouldn't go under the furniture and pick up the needles, so we had a hoover as well – a long sausage-like thing with a runner on it like a sledge.

We didn't have central heating, of course. There were fireplaces in all the rooms, but we didn't normally light them. But every Christmas we would stoke the fire up in the living room and my dad would take shovels of coal up into the little fireplaces in the bedrooms. We had to make sure that the coalman came just before Christmas, because we were going to use much more coal than usual. That was a Christmas treat, to have a fire in the bedroom.

But having those fires meant yet another job my mum had to do to prepare for Christmas. She'd cut any old clothes into strips and she'd get sacks from the greengrocer's – the old-fashioned hessian sacks that would have had potatoes in. We'd fold the sacking over and use a meat skewer to punch holes in it, then poke the strips of material through to make a rug. And these were the little hearth rugs we'd have in the bedrooms when we lit the fires at Christmas.

We also brought the Christmas trimmings out, decorations that were stored from year to year. We had lots of balloons, some of which had faces on and you never knew what they were going to look like until you blew them up. There was one that stood about three feet high and it had two cardboard feet, linked together but with a slot between them. When you blew it up it turned into Father Christmas – it must have been two or three balloons in one, because it certainly had something like a waistline. It took Dad ages to blow it up because of course he would blow and then stop to take a breath and some of the air would come out and he'd have to blow a bit more. And this was all done by mouth – there were no pumps to help him.

Once this Father Christmas was blown up, you couldn't tie a knot in it, because you'd never get it undone. So Dad used to have to hold the end stretched out while Mum wound lots of bits of string round it and pulled it ever so tight so that it didn't collapse. Then she slotted the string between the cardboard feet. Year after year that Father Christmas stood in a corner and when you went past you would knock it and it would wobble and bounce back. Then every year Mum and Dad would carefully let it down and pack it away for next Christmas.

We had silver and gold balls to hang on the tree, and there were two that had ladies' faces. They were very realistic – they even had hair moulded into the glass. Mum and her sister used to call them Mrs Brown, because when they were kids they'd known a lady called Mrs Brown who they said looked like these baubles. The balls had special clips on them, or loops that you would slot string through, so you could fix them to the branches, but we kids were never allowed to do that in case we broke anything. Dressing the tree was Mum and Dad's job.

We had fairy lights that were like little globes on a wire. My dad used to get these down – from the attic, I suppose – and lay them out on the floor, while my sister and I sat with our feet up so as not to get in the way of what he was doing. He would plug them in, which meant we couldn't have a lamp on, because you couldn't plug the lamp and the lights in at the same time. You couldn't have too many electrical appliances in those days because it would blow the system – that's one of the reasons we didn't have electric fires in the bedrooms.

Anyway, the lights would come on – orange and

yellow and green and blue, all the colours, it was very exciting. Then, having established that they worked, Dad would unplug them and drape them all round the tree, plug them back in again and they wouldn't work because he'd moved them. So he'd have to go along the string, tightening one bulb at a time and plugging them in again. Sometimes they'd work and sometimes they wouldn't – it was very touch and go. But when it did work it was magical.

Joan, with two small children to worry about, had to be careful:

We had an artificial Christmas tree, carefully stored from one year to the next, decorated with those very delicate trinkets that broke at the least little touch – icicles and balls mainly. We didn't have Christmas tree lights – the electricity would have been expensive – and I didn't want candles with small children around. We had hand-made paper decorations to hang from the ceiling. I got to be a dab hand at flour-and-water paste.

Sam remembers the excitement of going to his grandparents' house for Christmas:

My grandparents had decorations, quite elaborate ones, that they'd had for twenty or thirty years. They were the complete opposite of us. We had absolutely no money. My father worked hard, he just wasn't earning enough. But his father-in-law – my grandfather – had his own business, so they had lots of money, and shortages did not affect them to the same extent that they affected everybody else. My grandmother threw money at problems, because she had money to throw. She unashamedly bought things on the black market and we got stuff at her house that we wouldn't have anywhere else. She looked after her family in her own way; if she had to bribe somebody to get a little bit of special treatment, she would go ahead and bribe them. It didn't cross her mind that she was encouraging the black market; she was thinking of the family.

There were all sorts of lovely crepe paper decorations that you clipped together at the back and they made spheres of different colours, and bells – huge bells – that we hung from the ceiling and doorways and so on. And lots and lots of tinsel and fluffy strings of paper that you draped across the room. I think they'd had these since Edwardian times, but they were very decorative – I remember it quite well. It was good fun, but it took forever to get it all up.

We had an artificial tree, at home. It was metal and you folded down the branches so that you could put decorations on. My grandparents had a real tree – a big one, in the hall. The hall wasn't that big, though it seemed big to me as a tiny boy. It had a Morrison shelter in it and what with the tree and the shelter, there wasn't a lot of space left.

Ellie's recollections are similar but, living in a house with a large garden, her family was able to supplement the manufactured decorations:

We did have a small artificial Christmas tree, onto which we could clip small candleholders. These were then given tiny candles, which we lit every evening for a while. (We knew we couldn't get more, so they had to last.) How we managed never to start a fire amazed me then, and still amazes me now!

We put up paper decorations, which were kept from year to year, of course, same as we do these days. They were the ones that opened like concertinas and stretched across the sitting room, so two across the two diagonals decorated the room nicely. Also we had bells (concertina-style again), which were about nine inches in diameter when clipped shut. We had three holly bushes in the front garden, so we decorated the stairs with that. One dark green holly bush sometimes had red berries, a bonus. The other two bushes, one on either side, were green and yellow speckled, which made an interesting contrast, and if we dissolved some Epsom salts in a cup of hot water we could make quite realistic-looking 'frost' for the leaves.

Sue, born during the war, is another who remembers decorations that must have been stored up previously:

My grandmother had a Christmas tree, but at home we

had a branch rather than a whole tree. Trees were quite precious then, and I don't think people grew Christmas trees to sell in the way they do now. Our branch had lots of little branches coming off it, so when it was tied to a beam in the ceiling it hung down and looked like a tree. We had real little Christmas tree candles that you had to light, and old decorations that we hung on the tree. They must have been glass, because they were continually breaking, and of course that meant as the years went by there were fewer and fewer of them. Later on we learned to make silver stars, but at that time – when all three of us children were under six – it was just the glass things that had to be hung up carefully. Snow was little bits of cotton wool, which we would throw on to the branches. At the top we had a fairy – a tiny doll, about three inches long – with a white, rather yellowing skirt and wings made out of some shiny silky material. I don't know where it came from, but it certainly pre-dated the war.

Those 'real' candles form a large part of many people's memories. As more than one person observed, goodness knows what Health and Safety would make of that now. But some did take one practical precaution:

We always had a bag of sand in the living room, in case an incendiary bomb hit. And my mother kept a handbag by the front door, with all the insurance policies and ration books in it, so that she could grab it if we had to

CHAPTER 7

'FATHER CHRISTMAS HAD A LOT OF GREEN PAINT'

As with food, it took time for the impact of other shortages to be widely felt. In its Christmas issue for 1939, *Good Housekeeping* ran an article entitled 'Christmas as Usual'. Acknowledging that 'ingenuity and resource-fulness' would be needed to keep family and friends amused, it particularly advocated dressing up for the children (and gave an interesting insight into the sort of things its readers might be expected to have stashed away in the attic):

Mothers should collect a trunk or chest full of anything that holds possibilities in this direction. Discarded evening-dresses, ribbons, scarves, laces, beads and baubles, pieces of fur and lengths of material – in fact the wider the choice the greater the fun, and lucky indeed is the home that can boast, beg or borrow some old military or other uniforms.

When it came to presents, however, the magazine was sterner:

> Nobody wishes to waste money on the merely pretty or transitory thing, but even the useful gift can and should be a little festive. If possible, it should be something the recipient really needs, but which he or she would consider a slight extravagance to buy.

In the same month, *Country Life* magazine – presumably echoing the views of its upmarket clientele – conveyed the impression that the war was not much more than a bit of a nuisance, interfering with other pursuits. In its column 'Noted in Passing', it praised practical presents such as first-aid and gas-mask cases, but still found room to extol the virtues of a newly fashionable liqueur, Cointreau. With the blackout making shopping difficult, it also recommended catalogues issued by various department stores that were still able to offer 'nice goods in leather, toys, crackers, pretty eiderdowns and cushions' or 'lovely modern jewellery, extremely nice stationery and many other things'.

Even by 1939, however, toy retailers were noticing that the war was influencing the choice of presents: Harrods spoke of 'model trench scenes and troops in action…uniformed dolls and model ARP units', while Hamleys were selling 'a coastal defence gun which fired wooden shells' and scale models of Hurricanes and Spitfires, either in kit form or as made-up models.

From 1940 onwards, with shortages everywhere, buying Christmas presents became a struggle. Home-made was increasingly popular: a December edition of *Woman's Weekly* for 1940 gave patterns for a scarf – 'worked in a fine soft wool, it would make such a nice present' – and for 'Dobbin in crochet – such a lovable Christmas toy for a small boy or girl!' The following year its recommended toy was a knitted elephant; by 1942 it was horses again, this time made from oddments of wool.

Many children had to make do with a few small items left in the stocking or pillowcase at the end of their beds. More fortunate ones had both a stocking and a 'proper' present, but often only one. What presents there were, were simple – books, dolls, crayons and colouring books – and often second-hand. One woman remembered being given a penknife; another that she had received a potato peeler – and then had to spend half the morning using it as they prepared the vegetables for lunch. A lot of swapping and sharing went on. People whose children had grown out of clothes and toys passed them on to younger relatives or friends, or donated them to 'bring and buy' sales, where the parents of smaller children bought them cheaply.

Sue's family was fairly typical in this respect:

Our presents, without a doubt, would have been second-hand, from second-hand toyshops or somewhere like the Dolls' Hospital in Tunbridge Wells, which was our nearest big town. Or there were auctions in the village itself – people getting rid of toys their children had grown out of. Getting new toys was very, very rare. I know I had a tricycle the Christmas before the end of the war, when I would have been four, because there's a picture of me on it when we were evacuated to an uncle in Berkshire for the last four months or so of the war. (Bombs started to fall in our area then, which they hadn't before: when the doodlebugs started to come we got gun emplacements on the hill behind the village; they became a target and we children and our mother moved out for a little while.)

At home there were German prisoners of war working on farms nearby and I can remember them being taken through the village on the back of a tractor or a horse and cart. It was a small village, with very few children, and as it happens almost all of us were blonde. The prisoners were given coloured plastic thread to make things with and they used to give them to us as presents – little rings or bracelets, which they handed out with delight to these little fair-haired children, who must have reminded them of home. And of course we were delighted, too – I remember dancing round the cart calling, 'More, more!' We had no idea that these men were 'the enemy'.

One tradition we had at Christmas was to clear out our toy cupboard. It wasn't stuffed with a lot of toys because we simply didn't have a lot of toys. But it was a rule that we had to make room for any toys which we might, if we were very lucky and behaved very well, get on Christmas Day. The agony of saying goodbye to our precious toys! We handed them over to what was called the Christmas Crib – they were put round the crib in the church and then sent off, I think, to Barnardo's homes, or to children who were not getting presents. But we didn't like doing that.

Our presents weren't necessarily practical, but things like a tricycle, a scooter, a hobby horse – things we could play with, usually outside. Because we were so close in age we were a bit of a gang, and we'd be sent off to play in the garden or even further afield: it was perfectly safe because there were no cars. The occasional army vehicle or farm vehicle trundled through, but no one had a private car, or if they did it was up on bricks in the garage because of the shortage of petrol.

In Peterborough, Joan was one of many mothers who benefited from an informal recycling programme:

I remember we bought my son building bricks one Christmas – probably 1940, when he was three – and later we were given books, passed on by friends with older children. Like lots of small children at bedtime, my son would always demand another story, and then another, rather than go to sleep. Rupert Bear was a favourite, but there was one tale, 'Rupert and the Raven', which for some reason he didn't like. Perhaps the big black bird frightened him. Any time I thought he had had enough stories and it was time for him to go to sleep, I would suggest reading 'Rupert and the Raven'. 'No, thank you, Mummy,' he would say quickly, 'I think I'll go to sleep now.'

Christmas was definitely 'make do and mend'. For some reason we had been given a wooden box, and my son sat in it and imagined it was a boat; at other times he turned it upside down, sat on it and called it a train. Later, when my daughters were born, I made dolls for them by stuffing stockings or socks. Old hand-knitted jumpers were unravelled, the wool wound into skeins, washed, dried and rewound, and I used it to knit clothes for the girls and their dolls, and to make blankets for the dolls' cot that someone had given us.

But my son did have one unforgettable moment. A friend of his named June Boyall owned a three-wheeled cycle, and he really longed for one. We managed to get one second-hand, and I remember how delighted he was when we sent him into the front room on Christmas morning to see if Father Christmas had been. He came running back in great excitement and told us that Father Christmas 'had brought him June Boyall's bike!'

Other presents came to the same family in peculiar ways: Joan's father was a railway guard, working on a train that crossed the Duke of Gloucester's land, near Oundle:

The men who worked on the estate used to snare rabbits and sell them to the railwaymen – they'd hand them over when the train paused, waiting to go into the station. Sixpence each, they were – quite cheap, though you had to take them home and skin them and clean them yourself.

My dad had a friend who also worked on the railways: he would come out of Leicester on a train that passed Dad's coming out of Peterborough. He must have had a son who was older than mine, because when the two trains were due to pass each other, they slowed down so that Dad's friend could put his hand out of the window and hand something across. One time it was a few lead toy soldiers, another time it was a bag of marbles, but more than once that was the way my son got his Christmas presents.

Viv was another young mother who was grateful for any help she received:

My husband always said that people were kind to soldiers. That was probably because of this story, which he told often after the war.

He was in the army, stationed in Sheffield, and he was in a shop looking at children's handkerchiefs: he wanted a present for our little daughter. He didn't have the coupons that would allow him to buy them, and a lady standing next to him said to the salesperson, 'It's all right. I'll let him have the coupons.' I have no idea why she did that, but Julie got her Christmas present thanks to a stranger's generosity.

Sometimes presents came from an unusual source, as Pam remembers:

After the Italians surrendered, lots of them came to England as what they called 'co-operators' and worked on the land. There was a group of them in the fields near us in Gloucestershire. They were always singing and they seemed very cheerful, despite being more or less prisoners and working out of doors in a climate so much colder than their own. They were kind to us children, too: one Christmas they gave us oranges. They must have got these from their Red Cross parcels – there were certainly none for sale where we were.

Or there just weren't enough to go round. George was a pupil at the Foundling Hospital Schools in Berkhamsted:

I don't remember ever getting a present at Christmas, or any time like that. There used to be some presents come to the school that were supposed to be shared out, and I think that some of the real mothers, the birth mothers, sent things which weren't ever identified as coming from the mother. But they were shared out amongst us – there might be ten presents amongst thirty children.

As well as receiving things second-hand, swapping was a good way for children to get hold of things they longed for. Paper of all kinds was in short supply, which meant that some comics and magazines were published less frequently; others had fewer and/or smaller pages. Even the supply of school exercise books was strictly controlled. Children had to number the pages, so that it was not possible to tear out a page undetected. They also had to fill every line – teachers would check and make them go back and fill any blanks before issuing another.

Patterned wrapping paper gave way to brown paper and string, both of which people were exhorted to save and reuse. It also became vital not to throw out the scraps, which could be put to good use, as one magazine article explained: 'One old tie-on label from a parcel, for instance, will make the wads for forty rifle cartridges, and the snips of string will help to make the special paper for a navigation or gunnery chart.'

Advertisements urged 'Paper is precious! Don't let a day go by without making some contribution to the Paper Salvage Campaign!' and at Christmas in 1941, *Woman's Weekly* advocated a 'paper-clean' of the home as something every woman could do to help the country: 'old periodicals, old sheet music, old schoolbooks, old postcards, Christmas cards, old almanacks, cardboard boxes, wrappings and packings, old rolls of wallpaper, cardboard cartons and cigarette packets' should all be donated to the cause. The following year the magazine went a step further:

> I'll tell you a gift I am going to make – and that is a set of attractive chintz bags to hang on the door knob of each room for waste-paper, so that every scrap can be saved. Much more sensible to put paper into these bags than in a basket where it has to be sorted again from the other rubbish.

All this made comics good currency among the boys in the village where Tom was evacuated:

One Christmas, my parents sent me several copies of *The Beano*, and once I had read them I was able to swop them for *The Dandy* or *The Wizard*. Before the war I used to buy all three comics every week, but now because of the paper shortages they were published only once a fortnight, and tuppence a time mounted up to a lot of pocket money.

The comics kept us interested in the war effort, though. All my favourite characters were involved. The Wolf of Kabul in *The Wizard*, who usually worked for British Intelligence on the Northwest Frontier in India, took to plotting against the Nazis; even Lord Snooty in *The Beano*, who used to be happy just escaping from his castle to play in Ash Can Alley with his disreputable friends, started trying to thwart Hitler's plans.

Tony was another who relished comics and comic annuals:

Christmas was exciting when you were young – you got a lot of fun out of hanging your stocking up and writing out lists of things that you wanted, even if you knew you weren't going to get them: I always got either a *Beano*, a *Dandy* or a *Rupert* annual. But the things that I liked best of all were those colouring books where you just painted water on them. They were quite thick – pages and pages of line drawings – but when you painted them it was amazing, because all you needed was an eggcup with some water in it and a little paintbrush and then these pictures would just come to life.

I had some other wonderful presents, too. The most exciting thing I ever had was a John Bull Printing Outfit. There was a piece of wood, a sort of box with ridges in it, an ink pad and lots of tiny rubber capital letters, small letters, question marks, the lot. And there was a little pair of tweezers. The fascinating thing was working out how to slot these bits of rubber backwards into the ridges, so that when you turned the box over and stamped it out it made a word. I used to spend hours stamping out people's names and addresses. It was quite a big box and it must have been quite expensive. I think one of my aunts bought me that.

Bakelite was very popular in those days. Lots of things were made of it – practical things like radios and kitchen equipment. One year I was given a Bakelite tray with little boats in it. It must have been made specially for Christmas; I'm sure you couldn't have bought it any other time of the year. The boats were made out of Bakelite, different colours, and round the edge of the tray the Bakelite was moulded to form a harbour, with little steps. In between the boats there were sweets, and when you took the wrapping off and ate the sweets you could fill the tray with water and play with the boats as if it were a real harbour.

Less exciting – nearly every year I got a pair of slippers. I guess I grew out of them quickly and needed a new pair quite often. Mum belonged to the Co-operative Society, and nearly every week a man would come round and she would pay him two shillings [10p] or whatever she could afford. Every so often he would give her a card of five-shilling [25p] coupons which she could spend in the Co-op. That's how we got shoes and things like that.

The post office also ran a Christmas club. My mum used to send me up there with a threepenny bit every now and then. 'Just go up to the post office and put that on the club,' she'd say. So they'd write 'threepence' against your name in a book. Of course I didn't know what this was about, but at the end of the year it was buying my *Beano*, *Dandy* and *Rupert* annuals.

Comics weren't the only hobby, as Tom recalls:

Like many other children my age – I was nine when war broke out – I was a passionate stamp collector. My father was keen, too: he had a pair of Britain's first commemorative stamps, issued in 1924 to celebrate the British Empire Exhibition. He told me that King George V (also an avid philatelist) disapproved of the idea of commemorative stamps – I think he thought they were vulgar, or something that only foreigners would produce. But somehow or other His Majesty had been overruled, the commemorative issue was printed, and at Christmas 1939 my father passed those two stamps on to me as the start of my own collection.

No commemorative stamps were issued during the war – ink was in short supply, as well as paper, and wartime stamps were noticeably paler in colour because they used less ink. But I had an uncle in the RAF who had been stationed in Bermuda, and he brought me a series of their stamps. They were in different colours – the half-crown one was red, I remember, and the pound one was purple – but they all had a crown and a picture of King George VI. Bermuda sounded very exotic and exciting to me, and I couldn't understand why they had *our* king's head on *their* stamps. I remember all the adults laughing when I asked, but I couldn't help being a bit disappointed: I had an Australian stamp with a koala on it, and I had assumed that all stamps from the Empire would be like that.

For those who had the skills, there was the option of making toys, some of which were very special, as David recalls:

I was five when war broke out, living in Cardiff. My father was too ill to be in the Forces, but he was in the ARP, serving as an air-raid warden. He'd been all sorts of things in his life – a miner, a trawlerman, working on the scaffold at the steelworks – and he was very good with his hands. He used to make toys as Christmas presents and I would help paint them: forts, wobbling ducks with paddle feet, the kind you put on a slope and they waddled down. There was the occasional doll's house too. He gave them away to family and friends – it was a great help, because of course things like this were hard to come by, and most people couldn't afford them anyway. Presents would go round the tree – we always had a tree, a live one – not very big, but we had one.

Mike in Kent remembers being given a special present:

> Meccano usually came in a cardboard box, but my set was in a purpose-designed wooden box: my father had commissioned a local craftsman to make it. It was a magnificent piece of carpentry – beautifully detailed and lovingly finished. I went on to teach woodwork and other crafts for many years, then later I took up painting, and at the age of eighty am building a three-storey tree house for myself. I'm sure that Meccano set, and its box, sparked my interest in making things with my hands.

Brenda from Stockton-on-Tees also remembers 'bespoke' presents:

> My grandfather worked as a boilermaker in the shipyard, and he had a friend who was a carpenter. He made a farmyard and a crane for my brother and a set of doll's house furniture for me – all painted shipyard green. My brother said Father Christmas must have had a lot of green paint.
>
> I always looked forward to receiving a book at Christmas – I remember *Swallows and Amazons* and a Penguin book about pandas, but my favourite was my Shirley Temple book, with pictures of the child star in all her lovely outfits.

Joan's husband, stationed in Yeovil, created something special for his two small daughters:

He made two child-size painting easels and brought them home to Peterborough with him on the train, crossing London with them and his kitbag. Unlike most men, he didn't smoke during the war and gave his cigarette ration to other soldiers in exchange for chocolate, which he saved to bring home for the children.

Alfie remembers an unusual Christmas in 1944:

I don't think we celebrated Christmas much, but in 1944 for some reason my parents invited four German prisoners of war for Christmas lunch. What made it really special was that each of the Germans had made me a present. A toy soldier, a wooden train, things they had obviously built themselves. It was wonderful. I don't remember ever having a Christmas present before, and that year I had four!

In south London, Mollie's brother did his best:

During the war you couldn't get real wool to knit with (was it rationed too?), but you could get some awful hairy oily stuff. My brother learned to knit and knitted our dad a long scarf with lots of dropped stitches. He gave it to him for Christmas and insisted on him wearing it. It itched him to death. It was a sort of dirty, dull blue. I think Dad prayed his son would forget it quickly. But I do remember him wearing it to the football match. We used to watch Charlton Athletic playing at the Valley on Boxing Day. The swearing was quite strong and I'd pretend I'd not heard.

This was real parental devotion on the part of Mollie's dad – then, as now, Charlton played in red.

Knitting featured in other reminiscences too. Born in 1930, Jean was one of the youngest of a large family. Living in a village near Gatwick, which had become an RAF base when war broke out, she remembers getting advance warnings of air raids...

...because the soldiers used to know first. But one day we had a bomb and the shrapnel came right through our front door and knocked it sideways – it was left standing in the doorway at right angles to how it should have been. And it took the back off a mirror in the hall.

There were eleven children in my family, so we did all right for food – we could pool our ration books and buy bigger quantities. And there was a lady nearby who was quite rich – we used to give our clothing coupons to her and she would buy new clothes and pass second-hand things on to us. Mum would save them up and give them to us as Christmas and birthday presents. They were good clothes too, so as I say, we did all right.

We were living in a council block and we made our own air-raid shelter: just dug a pit and put tin across the top. No wonder we've got arthritis now, all that sitting on the damp ground. But we only went down the garden if it was really bad. My dad had a billiard table and we kids used to sleep lined up in rows under that, while my parents slept under the kitchen table. We'd sit there under the table knitting squares to make things for the troops. There was a special effort to produce things for Christmas – I guess the squares were made into blankets, and my mum and older sisters, who were better at knitting than I was, made socks and mufflers and things like that. But I have a clear picture of us sitting under the table knitting. We got used to it. We had mattresses under the table and when it was bedtime we just lay down and went to sleep.

Nora remembers a different kind of knitting:

There was this thing called Knitting Nancy. It was a little wooden doll, about four inches long, with a hole through the middle, like a long thin cotton reel. Or you could use an ordinary cotton reel. There were little metal hoops on the top and you somehow wound the wool round them. It was a bit like casting on for ordinary knitting – too complicated for small children, so your mother or your big sister did that bit for you. Then you had a hook and you hooked the wool over each hoop and pulled the tail of the wool out of the hole at the other end of the reel. So what you produced was like a long thin worm of knitting. You could coil it round and round and make things like mats and teapot stands with it. I suppose we sent those off to the troops, too – though why they needed loads and loads of teapot stands I don't know. I expect it was good for morale. But I certainly remember producing yards of the stuff, sitting in our Anderson shelter, waiting for the all-clear to sound.

Although parents went to a lot of trouble to make Christmas special, not all children were as grateful as they might have been. Albert remembers one present that baffles him to this day:

For some reason, in 1944, when I was six and my brother was eight, we were both given The Book of Common Prayer. I have no idea why. We were churchgoers, up to a point, but not to that extent. Perhaps it was celebrating that the war was about to end, but to us it hardly seemed the way to celebrate. Perhaps there had been a sale of second-hand books in the village, but you'd have thought there might have been more exciting books. It seemed very strange to both of us. But I remember my father had written 'To Albert, Christmas 1944' on the front page, and he had the most fantastic copperplate handwriting. I kept that book for a long time.

Ros wasn't so much ungrateful as terrified:

Even though he was only doing it for me – I was an only child – Dad went to the trouble of dressing up in a Father Christmas outfit to bring my stocking in after I had gone to bed on Christmas Eve. I'm sure parents used to do this in the hope that it would amuse the children for a while on Christmas morning, so they wouldn't get up too early and wake the parents. Anyway, I woke up one night to find Father Christmas in my bedroom. I was panic-stricken and hid under the covers until I heard him go away. My father laughed and laughed when I told him about this; it was years before I realised why.

Alternatively, longed-for presents could bring disaster. Beryl had a bad experience when she was very small:

I remember I desperately wanted a doll that walked – they were a new invention and I think you had to wind them up. But I had seen one in the toy shop. It had a most beautiful face, one of those china faces, with a very pretty complexion. And I was given one. At the time I was my parents' only child and if I wanted something that they could afford, they gave it to me. On Christmas morning, I made that doll walk and she fell down and her pretty face broke. I've never forgotten that – my lovely doll!

Val's experience with a doll was happier. She lived on a farm in southwest Scotland:

There was no holiday on the farm as animals still had to be fed, but somehow it was different because of that magical word Christmas. My sister and I sat in bed on Christmas morning emptying our stockings and being very excited about their meagre contents. We were given a book or jigsaw to share, but my most exciting present was a reversible dressed cotton dolly, fair-haired on one side and dark-haired on the other. The long skirt was a different pattern on each side and covered up the fact that the doll had two heads and no legs.

Maureen, too, remembers the excitement of being given a doll. She came from a large family and shared a bed with a number of her sisters:

I was the eighth of fourteen children, so I had several older sisters. We little ones would go to bed on Christmas Eve and hang our stockings over the end of the bed; then the older girls would creep up and collect them, take them downstairs, fill them and bring them back. We'd get an orange in the toe, a couple of nuts perhaps, and then one bigger present. If there was something we'd wanted during the year and our parents couldn't afford to buy it, they'd save up and try to get it for us for Christmas.

The thing that I really wanted was a black doll. Mother said I was too old to have dolls – I think I was twelve – and I was ever so upset about it. But on Christmas Eve I was awake when my sisters brought the stockings back. I lay there quietly until they'd done, but then I looked and I saw this little thing with a pink dress on and I knew it was my black doll. So I took it out and put it in bed with me, cuddled up to it and went to sleep.

In the morning, there was another doll in there. Another of my sisters, a little older than me, had been sitting up in bed at night-time, unknown to us, making me a rag doll. I don't know where she got the bits and pieces from, but she'd dressed it and put wool on it to make hair, and made it a face. And all because my mother had said I was too old to be given a doll. It was lovely, that rag doll – I loved it. I loved the black doll too, and I still had it on my bed when I got married. So I had two dolls that Christmas when I shouldn't have had any.

Barry is another who recalls a Christmas present that went wrong:

One present that was passed down from an older cousin was a pair of roller skates. I was eleven and had just finished my first term at the grammar school, so when I went out on Christmas afternoon to try out the skates I put on the warmest jacket I had – my school blazer. It was icy and I'd never skated before, so inevitably I fell and broke my arm. I remember my mother insisting that I take the blazer off before we went to the doctor's: he would just have slit the sleeve to get at my arm, and the blazer was too expensive to be damaged in that way! I'm sure it was two sizes too big for me and had been bought to last me most of my school career.

Even worse, Annie paid the penalty for misbehaviour:

My mother was very strict but I was naughty and rebellious. During the war my father was away and we didn't have much money and it must have been very hard for her, but that didn't stop me. One time just before Christmas I must have been particularly cheeky and my mother said, 'If you go on like that, you'll find cinders in your stocking on Christmas morning.'

'I don't care,' I said, but my mother was as good as her word – I woke up on Christmas Day to find my stocking was full of cinders. It took a lot of effort to say 'I don't care' that day.

On a happier note, Tony remembers some special sweets:

There were extra sweets in the shops: even during the war there were special things that you could only get at Christmas. Sometimes we'd get a little packet of chocolate Father Christmases. One thing I always got in my stocking was a packet of cigarettes, made out of a sort of soft rock, like hardened icing. They were white and the ends were red, as if they were lit. Twenty cigarettes in a little packet. That was a lot of sweeties, by the standard of those days.

There was a sweet shop in the town and at Christmas they made special ones, fruit flavoured. You could take a two-pound bag of sugar in – you had to save your coupons to do that. They'd give you a ticket and you'd go back the following week and collect a bag of hard-boiled sweets. You had to pay for them, though. They used your sugar rations, but they still took your money for the sweets.

Joyce remembers another sweet treat that appeared in Christmas stockings: 'sugar mice – a pink one and a white one, with a bit of a string for a tail.'

Spending money on presents could involve a lot of soul-searching. Evelyn wrote from Kendal in the Lake District to her husband Ernest. He was stationed in Sheffield – a long way to travel in wartime, when leave was as hard to come by as everything else – and she was anxious to keep him informed about the family's activities:

> *I think I shall post your Christmas present under registered post, about next Tuesday, or Wednesday. What do you think? Shall I send you half a cake? Have you anywhere to keep it? I did tell you that I had ordered a black-board and easel from the Co-operative, for Jeanne, didn't I? I shall get chalks, a box of pencil crayons each, and a box of Plasticine each. All things that please both greatly. I'm hoping somebody buys Michael just one substantial toy. Helen says she hopes to get him a railway set. If she does, that will put him right. He is 'full' of Christmas.*

She faced a hazardous journey to visit her mother for Christmas, but Helen, her niece, obviously came up trumps. The doll mentioned below, priced at seven shillings and ninepence (about 39p – a lot of money for a toy), must have been a special one:

> *If you advise me to go, I shall pack-up all luggage and children's Christmas 'things' and shall get them 'off' by*

Wednesday, by Rail. I shall have nothing but the children to attend to. Perhaps, though, I ought to carry the toys because there's always the danger of delay, and the 'blossoms' must have their Christmas. In addition to the doll (7/9!!!) and the Railway set, Helen bought a big box of lovely crackers with hats, 'jewels' and jokes in.

A few days later, Evelyn wrote again, enclosing her Christmas present to Ernest:

A very peaceful Christmas to you, and a watch to while away the hours to your safe return to me! I do so hope you will be happy to receive it because it has given me such happiness to buy it for you. And heavens! What time and energy I have spent in the choosing of it. Every Jeweller's shop in Kendal I went into, and every Jeweller I eyed with suspicion, so much so that I gave up the quest and decided to buy you some suspenders. However, I related my 'tale of woe' to Mrs Knipe who advised me to go to a family friend and watch-dealer, etc., etc., and suggested I mentioned her name. Of course, once entering upon the business, I became 'weaker' than ever (No, darling I didn't fall for the heaven-sent watch-maker), I merely fell more deeply for you, and spent twice as much as I had intended. But there you are! I always mean to give you the best or nothing, and you're worth it. You will see the watch is not a 'flashy' chromium one. It is <u>solid</u> silver and carries a good guarantee. I chose the round faced one because I'm given to understand the oblong ones are

difficult to replace if broken. Now, if anything goes wrong,
let me have it back. When you come home, I shall have
your initials worked on the back. I could not get this done
in time for Christmas.

Suspenders, in this context, were braces: for holding up
trousers rather than stockings.

In the course of 1941 Ernest was posted to Egypt, but he
managed to send Christmas presents home. Evelyn responded:

Dearest,
'Cherubs' thrilled to receive their presents. Jeanne says doll
is best she has ever seen. Michael almost beyond himself
with football. Now, I dare not enter dining-room without
first 'ducking' my head. Very sad to say I have not yet
received my scarf. Since I have had 4 letters, Hilda 1 &
Dr Cockill 1 apparently on the same boat as children's
toys, feel convinced that scarf should have been along. If
it does not turn up I shall swear it has either not been
sent by shop-people or it has been 'pinched' in England.
It must have come along, if at all, by same boat. I have
never wanted anything so much in all my life before.

Did it turn up? Sadly, we shall never know.

Mabel, living in Coventry, wrote frequently to her husband
in Egypt. Prior to this letter, written on Christmas Day 1942,
she had mentioned longingly the recipe book she describes
here. She had been going to suggest that her mother bought
it for her, but worried it would be too expensive. Instead

perhaps she would have it as her husband's present to herself, or hers to him, as it would be bought with his stomach in mind. Clearly, even such a modest purchase as a recipe book was a great extravagance for many people.

I bought Mum some flowers but not many as they are terribly expensive, but didn't get anything else as neither Mum or I could think of anything to get, so are waiting until she wants something. I had the recipe book from Mum as I told you… Your Mum gave me an engagement calendar and some chocolate, and by post this morning a note case from Eileen. She says she knows I have 'tons of notes, but has never seen me using a case'. Actually it was something I particularly wanted, each time I look at the shops I've been tempted to buy one, but have not felt justified in spending the money and I'm glad now I didn't…

Judy, aged twelve at the start of the war, remembers that her large extended family found a way of giving everyone a treat. They would all provide two presents, each costing no more than ten shillings [50p]:

Ten shillings was a lot of money for us children, so we were allowed to cheat a little: you could buy something like a Dinky Toy car for about four shillings [20p], and my little brother and my three cousins would all have been delighted with that. I think my dad somehow managed to give us extra pocket money in the week we were doing our shopping. Lots of the presents were home-made: one of my aunts had an apple tree and a plum tree in the garden, and she used to give out bottled fruit; another did very pretty embroidery. We wrapped everything up in newspaper, put the presents in my mother's big basket and had a lucky dip. Not everything was suitable for everyone, of course, so we were allowed to swap, but I remember it being very exciting.

Most exciting of all was the Christmas when I received a large bar of Lux toilet soap. Not just the ordinary size – a LARGE one. Like so many other things, soap was rationed: you got four coupons every four weeks to cover all soap products – including what you used for washing yourself, your clothes and your hair; shampoo was a real luxury and bubble bath unheard of. That Christmas present would have cost two coupons – two weeks' worth! – so it was very generous of whoever contributed it to our lucky dip.

Plus it was Lux. We thought Lux was very glamorous because Judy Garland advertised it in magazines: 'Here's Judy Garland…young and lovely…here's the beauty soap she uses every day.' And I suppose we believed it – Judy Garland certainly was lovely, and I thought she was extra special because she had the same name as me. I would have been fifteen or sixteen by this time and it seemed important. Lux had a whole campaign exploiting our love of film stars: Deanna Durbin, who played lots of young and innocent girls-next-door, also advertised it, and Betty Grable, 'the girl with the million-dollar legs', was said to wash her nylons in Lux flakes. There wasn't much to make us feel glamorous in 1943 or '44, so we grabbed what we could, and if kidding ourselves we were copying the film stars made us feel better, then I guess we were happy to kid ourselves. I know I was.

Mary from Gravesend gives perhaps the best summary of how happy people could be with very little during the war:

I don't remember much about Christmas, but I know we did celebrate it, because I can remember finding an apple and an orange at the bottom of a stocking, or a tiny chocolate thing. Now you'd think nothing of it, but then – I can't tell you what a wonderful feeling it was, to find those things at the foot of the bed.

And Dolly remembers that, war or no war, parents could make their children's Christmas entrancing:

When we went to bed on Christmas Eve, our front room was just the way it was every other day. Then my mother and grandmother would set to and make mince pies while Dad put up the Christmas tree and decorated the room. They'd hang up our stockings and put little bits and pieces in them – Dad had a way of twisting a piece of paper into a cone to put sweets in. On the floor below them they'd put our present. So we children would come down on Christmas morning, when it was still dark, and all this had been done and the candles had been lit on the tree – and it was magical.

CHAPTER 8

'GOOD, CLEAN, INNOCENT FUN'

In the absence of television, radio was the primary entertainment during a quiet evening at home – and that
meant either the BBC Home Service (the forerunner of Radio
4) or, from January 1940, their light-entertainment Forces
Programme. On Christmas Eve 1939 the Home Service
offered various concerts, including the Carol Service from
King's College Cambridge; a seasonal drama, 'Christmas
at Dingley Dell', adapted from Dickens' *Pickwick Papers*;
and, as a perfect piece of escapism just before bedtime,
P. G. Wodehouse's *The Crime Wave at Blandings*. Its hero,
the unworldly Lord Emsworth, would certainly have been
concerned if someone tried to steal his prize pig, but was
unlikely to have been aware that there was a war on.

A year later there was music of every kind, but also
Impersonations, described as 'a parlour lark'. In 1942

the regular programme *What I'm Reading Now* featured Christmas books, while bedtime fare was a reminiscence by the biologist Julian Huxley, Secretary of the Zoological Society of London, of the famously gaffe-prone Dr William Spooner, whom he had known at Oxford.

For those who owned a piano, there were also sing-songs to be had. Tony even managed some special effects:

It was an upright piano and I used to take the front panel off, exposing the hammers. Then I'd put tissue paper between the hammers and the wires and produce a honky-tonk sort of noise. My father was very musical and it used to drive him mad, but it was fun for sing-songs at Christmas.

Ros remembers:

I had quite a good singing voice and I was used to singing in the choir at church and Sunday School. I remember having a solo of 'The Holy City', the one that Charlotte Church recorded a few years ago, with the chorus that goes:

Jerusalem! Jerusalem!
Lift up your gates and sing,
Hosanna in the highest!
Hosanna to your King!

It was a Victorian song, but Jeanette MacDonald had sung it in a film just before the war, so it was popular again. It had some very high notes – I couldn't hit them now. Our domestic 'Christmas concerts' took place next door at my uncle and aunt's place because they had a piano. Auntie Hetty always used to lead the singing, but one year she must have had a cold and I was asked to take over. She had been a great fan of Marie Lloyd, the music-hall singer, so she always used to sing her songs – 'My Old Man Said Follow the Van', and the one that became my favourite, 'The Boy I Love is Up in the Gallery'. There was nothing very Christmassy about it, except the line 'As merry as a robin that sings on a tree', but we all used to join in. When I grew up I used to perform in old-time music halls, and over the years I must have sung that song hundreds of times, but I always associate it with Christmas in Auntie Hetty's living room.

A number of Pauline's relations were also talented musicians. They were part of a concert party that at Christmas would perform at the local Labour Club and other venues round about:

My aunt had a really good voice and had been in Ivor Novello's shows. At home at Christmas, Grandad always played the piano and they sang songs like 'Old Father Thames Keeps Rolling Along'. Grandad and one of my uncles both thought they were comedians, and after dinner they used to come out with the jokes. One of the things they used to do was tell my grandmother that they were going to take the piano upstairs.

'No, no, no,' she'd say, 'I don't want the piano upstairs.'

Well, the one they insisted on moving was an imaginary piano – a grand piano. They'd get round it and say things like, 'Up your end', 'He's got it on my foot', and make out they were carrying this imaginary piano upstairs. And my grandmother used to sigh and say, 'Oh, you children. I don't know.' She said children, but my uncles were all in their thirties by then, they just liked messing about.

We played games too – we used to bob for apples, putting apples into a bowl of water and trying to pick them up in our teeth. And there was another game where you laid a bottle down on its side and sat on it with your feet up – you had to keep your legs stretched out in front of you and your ankles crossed. You'd have a pack of cigarettes to one side and a box of matches to the other and you had to lean over and pick them up and light the cigarette without falling off the bottle. You could never do it, of course, because you couldn't keep your balance on the bottle.

Nancy remembers singing, but also card games:

We had a wind-up gramophone and a few records, but mostly we sang round the piano. 'Run, Rabbit, Run' and 'We're Going to Hang Out the Washing on the Siegfried Line' were popular, and of course anything by Vera Lynn. 'We'll Meet Again', that was my favourite.

After Christmas lunch we'd play charades or cards – Nap and Newmarket were the games, and we played for pennies. We had a big mirror in the sitting room and my brother was naughty; Dad always sat with his back to the mirror and my brother used to say, 'Hold your cards up, Dad', so he could see a reflection of what my father had in his hand.

Nap isn't as popular now as it once was, but Nancy's wasn't the only family that used to play it. Pam from Bolton remembers:

We used to play Nap at Christmas, and only at Christmas. I suppose it's because it's a good game for six or eight people, and Christmas was the one time that the whole family got together. It's a sort of mini-whist, and you call how many tricks you think you are going to take. One of the highest calls is 'Nap' or 'Napoleon', which – reasonably enough, if you know your history – can only be beaten by 'Wellington'. My Uncle Len, who got a bit riotous after two glasses of port, always used to insist that we called 'Hit' (for Hitler) and 'Church' (for Churchill) instead. He said that if we were going to be patriotic, we ought to be up to date about it.

Newmarket was also good with large numbers. Pam again:

The thing about Newmarket was that you didn't need to be a good card player, so it was great for us children.

As long as you were old enough to understand that you had to put the four of hearts on top of the three of hearts, you could play. But if you were a bit older and a bit more cunning, you could make life easy or difficult for other players. I remember the Christmas that I was nine, my father was home on leave for the first time in months and I did everything I could to help him to win. My brother and cousin were furious – they were older and much more hard-nosed than I was; I was just so happy to have Daddy home that I wanted everything to be nice for him.

Sue's family had a different game:

After lunch, we played a game called Up Jenkins. We all had to sit round the table and secretly pass a coin round – it was either a farthing or a silver threepenny bit. We had to hold our fists out in front of us and somebody would guess who was holding the coin. If they guessed you, you had to open your hands and if the coin fell out you lost a life.

There were well-known board games such as Ludo and snakes and ladders, and other diversions that came into their own when lots of relations came round. Sam remembers:

The things I recall playing with include stuff from my grandparents' or parents' era, such as pinball games ('Corinthian'?) and something similar to shove ha'penny, but activated by a wire strung across the bottom of the board. These tended to be dug out from an under-stairs cupboard at Christmas and other times when cousins arrived and we all needed to be kept amused.

Betty played something similar, a game called Bagatelle:

It was a large wooden rectangle with one rounded end, and lots of little nails stuck in the board, making horseshoe shapes. You shot metal balls round the board with a plunger, like on a pub pinball machine, and the idea was to get the balls to sit in the horseshoes and score points. I haven't seen it for years, but we used to play it all the time at Christmas. The only problem was that you had to take it in turns, and my little sister wasn't always very good at waiting till I had finished.

Ellie also remembers more creative activities:

After the meal we played games with the adults – hide-and-seek, charades, hunt the thimble, consequences (where each person writes an opening statement on a piece of paper, then folds it over and passes it on; the next person has to add another statement without seeing the first one, and folds it over and so on. Some of the slips were really funny when read out at the end.) All good clean innocent fun.

Good clean fun while the children were around, perhaps, but

consequences could degenerate into something more riotous later in the evening, as Ken recalls:

> The rules of the game went something like this: the first person wrote down the name of a man, the second the name of a woman, the third the place where they met. The paper was folded over each time so that no one knew what had been written before. Next came 'he said to her', then 'she said to him' and finally 'and the consequence was'. We'd had a particularly prim great-aunt – Maud, her name was – who had died just before the war, and let's just say we didn't always remember her with great respect. It was extraordinary how many games of consequences involved Aunt Maud meeting the milkman, the butcher's boy and even, once, Errol Flynn.

But as Stan pointed out, sometimes it wasn't so much what you did as the fact that you did it:

> I don't generally have much memory of Christmas during the war. I was living in Beckenham in Kent, and we were close to Biggin Hill airfield, which was a constant target, and used to seeing masses of planes in the air. I remember once – it must have been during the Battle of Britain – seeing about five hundred German planes at once. It was a glorious day and they were like silver fish in the sky, until the fighters got in amongst them and then it was chaos. Another time I remember seeing a pilot bale out of a plane and land in someone's garden while his plane

went on and crashed into some houses further down the road. Then from 1944 we were very much 'flying bomb alley', with lots of V-1s coming through. So with all these things going on, Christmas was just another day.

But I do remember Christmas 1944. I was in the Sea Cadet Corps, waiting to join the navy, and we'd planned a party. Nothing special in the way of food and drink – just a bit of a get-together for a few friends waiting to be called up. Well, the day before the party our headquarters were bombed, and I remember frantic arrangements for temporary accommodation being made so that we would have somewhere to hold the party. The important thing was just to carry on.

Not many people could afford any kind of party. Dorothy remembers taking pity on local children who couldn't expect much in the way of celebration at Christmas:

I was working for the water authority – I'd begun as a shorthand typist, but the four men in the office were all called up and they made me do their jobs; they got another girl in to do the shorthand typing and I ended up managing the department. There was a girl keeping the books, and she and I decided that the local children weren't likely to have much of a Christmas, so we'd hire a hall nearby and give them a party. We worked like billy-o and then we fretted in case they didn't come.

We needn't have worried. The hall was up a little lane and on the day that lane was full from the bottom to the top. We'd put a sign up in the office and we were expecting the children of all our employees, but word had obviously got around – there must have been at least a hundred of them. We had a lot of tables laid out with home-made cakes that we had begged and borrowed. I don't know how we managed to put it together, but we did; people must have hoarded their sugar rations to do all that baking. And we made lots of lemon squash – you could buy the concentrate, same as you can now, and make it up with water.

The girl who was helping me, the book-keeper, was married to a policeman, who came to help us. If it hadn't been for him it would have been utter chaos. He organised the children – he had the size and the authority to keep them more or less under control. I remember I was standing on one side of a table and it was coming towards me, with the pressure of the children. I thought I was going to be pushed over. It was the shock of my life to see those children, the sheer numbers of them, because they simply weren't having parties otherwise.

In an anthology of Christmas memories published in the forties, Helen Hardinge, whose husband was private secretary to King George VI, recalled something a bit grander. The princesses she mentions were the future Queen Elizabeth II and her sister, the Princess Margaret:

After the war came, there were many changes in all our lives, and especially many changes at Christmas; the time for rejoicing was taken away. But during those most strenuous years there were one or two moments when it was possible to revive a little of the happiness that should belong to the festival. Some children had been forced to remain in London, in spite of the exodus of all their companions. St. Martin-in-the-Fields, that most all-embracing of churches, had gathered in these poor small wanderers, looked after them, taught them, and done what it could to see that they were safe on the streets of London; and one year at Christmas time with the help of those who minister at St. Martin's, I had a tree at St. James's Palace, a really lovely tree, in spite of the war, and a source of great enjoyment to myself as well as to them. The lights were lit once more for a short time round this symbol of Christ's nativity; and, as we were able to bring to the children a little of what was good in the old unaltered ways, so they brought joy to us. We played games afterwards, slipping about on the rather bare, shiny floors, from which so much of the furniture had gone. And then when it was all over, there was a great deal of washing-up to do; but somehow the brightness of that evening never faded or got dimmed, even by fatigue at the sink.

Then, during the war, a Christmas pantomime was inaugurated at Windsor Castle, to raise funds for the Merchant Navy, and everyone helped in this – not only by subscribing, but also by taking an active part, where needed, to assist the producer and performers; to paint scenery, or to play in the band, or to help with the costumes. The principal actors were the Princesses, friends of theirs from the locality, and the village schoolchildren, many of whom had come down from London and joined the local school for the war. They were all treated as performers and actors, not as people of any particular class – and indeed, they were of all classes; there is nothing like a good dramatic performance, where your achievement is all that counts, to extinguish any class-consciousness. Of all these occasions, the one I loved most was the Nativity Play, which was put on in St. George's Hall, that great long gallery, with its huge windows lighting up the Garter Shields which ornament the room. There was a raised dais at the end of the room where the play took place. It was beautifully produced: the singing was exquisite, and the ancient drama itself vivid and fresh. This took place at a very bad time during the war, and was a deeply moving presentation. The most striking moment was when the 'Three Kings' came in procession, walking up the length of the hall, with Princess Elizabeth leading them. She was dressed in the pageantry of ancient kingship, and carried a most beautiful casket of figured gold, which had been lent her by her mother; she moved with beauty and nobility to offer this to the infant Christ. A deep emotion was felt by the audience; and at the end, everyone was snivelling away and swallowing lumps in the throat, and generally presenting an unsightly and shamefaced appearance as they furtively dabbed at their faces. Somebody said: 'There's hardly a dry eye in this hall,' and the Queen said:

'I know, it is such a wonderful old story.' But the feeling was more complicated than that: a deeper sense of the present, and of how much we had to lose if the dark hour of the outer world engulfed us – a sense of the beauty of all we cherished most.

Joan, from a village in Suffolk, took part in a pantomime on a smaller scale:

The annual pantomime was a big event, held in the village hall and with most of the village people joining in. When I was about eight, I played Buttons, and I wore a little red suit with round gold buttons. I don't know who made it, but it must have been cut down from a much bigger dress – we wouldn't have been able to get material to make it from new.

I remember I sang a duet with my sister Joyce:

I'm a little prairie flower
Dancing out at every hour
Nobody cares at all about me
But I'm as wild as wild can be.

Then there was a bit where we had to march and sing:

This is the army, Mr Jones
No private rooms or telephones
You had your breakfast in bed before
But you won't have it there any more.

We lived perhaps a couple of miles outside the village and we used to go to somebody's house in the village for rehearsals, and we heard this doodlebug. The doodlebugs made a distinctive put-put-put noise, and we used to run outside to watch them. You'd see a light – it was the flame coming out of the back – and then the noise would stop. This time when it stopped my mother said, 'That's right over our house. We've got to get home, quick,' because Dad and Jock – that was the dog – were there. Fortunately the bomb came down in a field, about a mile away, and nobody was hurt.

For young adults, entertainment outside the home meant cinemas and dance halls. Martha, in her twenties, remembers that all leave was something to savour, and Christmas leave in particular:

I had four days off over Christmas once – and only once, during the war. That may not sound much nowadays, when almost everything shuts down between Christmas and New Year, but back then it was an incredible luxury. I was in the ATS, working as a truck mechanic, and I seemed to be dirty all the time. So it was a real treat, not only to be out of uniform but to have the prospect of cleaning my fingernails – and keeping them clean for a few days. Make-up was hard to come by and expensive; I remember teasing the last scrapings of lipstick out of the bottom of the tube with the blunt end of a pencil, knowing that when that ran out I'd probably be reduced to colouring my lips with beetroot juice.

The slogan 'Save money and metal' was coined to encourage women to take their lipstick containers into shops or the local NAAFI for refilling. Cosmetics became eye-catchingly patriotic, notably Helena Rubinstein's 'Regimental Red' lipstick – 'ideal against subdued khaki and service blues' – and Tangee's Natural 'Uniform' range, because 'on duty you must look smart – but never painted'. The problem was, you couldn't rely on these products being in the shops when you wanted them. Martha continues:

I was also one of many who drew seams on my bare legs with potassium permanganate, to make it look as if I was wearing nylon stockings, because in those days nylons had seams up the back. Once they became fashionable – after the Americans arrived – no one would be seen dead in the old lisle stockings we'd worn before that, certainly not on a night out. The alternative to lisle had been silk, which I certainly couldn't afford. It was much better to paint on a seam and freeze if need be. My mum always had potassium permanganate in the bathroom cabinet – you used it to treat dermatitis and things like that – and I would sneak in and 'borrow' some. Looking back, I imagine she knew perfectly well what I was doing, but she never let on. And anything I did to make myself look better, I could always tell myself – and my mum – that

I was doing it for the morale of the troops! In the early days of the war there was a lot of propaganda about that: the fashion magazines were full of articles about how women should keep themselves looking good for the benefit of their menfolk.

Maintaining your looks was indeed a recurring theme in women's magazines: in December 1940 the *Woman's Own* beauty pages had this to say:

Yes, I know you think Christmas won't be Christmas this year, but believe me Christmas always is Christmas, and more so when there is a boy coming home on leave. Try to look festive. It's your duty to yourself, to your country and to the boy friend.

One of the suggested ways of looking festive was to use sequins to smarten up 'shoes that haven't danced for ages' – and to stick one or two on your face to match. Less frivolously, the magazine's beauty expert beseeched readers to shampoo their hair and rinse it very thoroughly to make it shine, and to try her rejuvenating skin treatment, 'because judging from some of the faces I see looking at me a great many people need it'.

Whether or not you stuck sequins on your shoes, going out bare-legged was seen by an older generation as a bit 'fast', so painting the legs to mimic the colour of stockings was another fashion option. Various cosmetic companies produced lotions designed to simulate a suntan, but they were expensive. Martha again:

I had dark hair and quite dark skin, so I didn't mind so much, but I had two very fair-skinned friends – two sisters – who were always worrying that their legs looked pale and blotchy, which wasn't what they wanted when they were going dancing. They used to sponge them all over with diluted gravy browning or cocoa, which was fine as long as you didn't get caught in the rain. If you did, the brown 'make-up' would run all over the place. You could buy cheaper versions of the commercial brands, but they had a tendency to make your legs glow yellow under the lights in a dance hall. Again, not the glamorous look we were striving for.

We spent a lot of time at the Paramount Ballroom in Tottenham Court Road. There were always lots of American servicemen there, and they taught us a new dance called the jitterbug. It was really exhilarating – the more adventurous partners would throw you over their shoulders, so you exposed a lot of leg and even a bit of knicker. Not the sort of thing you told your mum about! I remember being there during that Christmas leave and hearing the air-raid warnings go off. Of course we should all have headed down to the shelters straight away, but we just kept on dancing. Fortunately no one dropped a bomb near us that night, or a lot of people would have been killed.

Much the same attitude prevailed at the cinema, where it was quite common for a sign to flash across the screen: 'A siren has been sounded. Anyone wishing to stay in the

CHAPTER 9

'THE BIG REMINDER OF THE HORRORS OF THE WAR'

For those who believed, and even for many who didn't, church was an important part of Christmas and a way of holding a community together. Prayers were said for the safety of those in danger and for the comfort of the anxious and bereaved; they were particularly poignant when they referred to your own friends and neighbours.

John's father had been the rector at a village in Hampshire. He retired in 1933 and the family moved to Oxford:

We had always been churchgoers, but there were many more people in church on Christmas Day during the war. The services were rather sad, with people praying for their loved ones and for an end to all the awful things that were happening. From 1940 until 1943, there were no bells: it had been decreed that church bells would be rung only to indicate that a German invasion was imminent.

We did go carol singing, though, wandering through the streets of Oxford with tiny lanterns or torches, covered so that their light was directed on the ground. We would tap on people's doors if they hadn't already come out when they heard us. A lot of money was collected for charity that way.

Stephen remembers bell-ringing as one of the many things that just 'weren't the same' during the war:

We'd been allowed to ring the bells only once – after Monty's victory at El Alamein in November 1942. Then the government decided that regular bell-ringing could resume on 25 April – Easter Sunday – 1943, because the threat of air raids had diminished. But there simply weren't enough of us to do it properly. We rang the bells on Sunday mornings from then on, but there were usually only three of us – those of the pre-war ringers who were too old or too young to have been called up – and eight bells to deal with. It wasn't great bell-ringing, but it was wonderful to be able to make some sort of sound after nearly three years of silence.

For Aldwyn's family, music was particularly important:

As a family we were regular worshippers at the 'all Welsh' non-conformist chapel. Unlike the Church of

England, we had no special services on Christmas Day. There were three chapels in the village (Methodist, Baptist and Congregational) and to celebrate Christmas we had a Cymanfa Ganu – a combined service of song when specially chosen Welsh hymns and anthems would be sung, conducted by some eminent musician from one of the other valleys. This took place on the Sunday nearest to Christmas Day. There would be three services in the course of the day – morning, afternoon and evening – and the three chapels took it in turns to host them. Each service would include the combined singing of the three congregations and some solos and readings. During my childhood before the war, and in the years during and immediately after it, I think Welsh chapel singing was at its strongest, most powerful and uplifting.

Nancy remembers Christmas services in her home village:

Going to church was the big reminder of the horrors of the war: we prayed for the young men in the Forces, mentioning the ones from our villages by name because we knew them all. That was always special. You have to remember that it was a different world then: our outlook on life was very different from what it is now. There was no pouring out your feelings on Facebook or anywhere else. We weren't sentimental – we hadn't been taught to be sentimental. We just got on with living and made the best of everything.

As early as 1939, Jean, a vicar's daughter in her teens, remembers not being able to hold the Christmas Eve carol service:

> At home we had blackout curtains in the main rooms and cardboard tacked over the window in the kitchen, but there was no way we could cover the huge stained-glass windows in the church. That meant that all services had to be held in daylight, and the weather that first winter of the war was dreadful; some days it barely got light at all. The only consolation was that Westminster Abbey was in the same boat – their choir boys had been evacuated, so they had to cancel their carol service, too.

The blackout caused Rose some consternation on Christmas morning when she got up early to go to church. She wrote in her diary:

> *Got down there by 8. The Church was in darkness and seemed deserted, but then I heard a little cough down on the right front, and then a little one on the left front, so I thought there must be some other people there, so I just waited. Then someone came up the aisle with a torch and said something to a man over on the left hand side, which I took to be the Service was cancelled. Anyway the man disappeared, and the Church was absolutely deserted, so after sitting there for a little while I thought I had better go, but before going, I thought I would investigate a little glimmer of light down on the left hand side of the altar.*

So I did, and found a tiny little service going on there in what is I suppose the choir boys' and clergymen's cloak room. There were pegs etc. all round and oddments you usually find there. We had the full service there, about 30–40 people I suppose, and it reminded me very much of Cromwell's time or the Reformation time, and the way people had to have their services in secret, and the priest's hole and everything.

Roy remembers being packed off to church on Christmas morning:

I didn't want to go, but my parents insisted it was the right thing to do, so off I went and the church was packed. It was a big church and I can remember it being freezing cold; I sat there and shivered all through the service. I had no interest in what was going on. But for a lot of other people, church was a great solace – a consolation.

Joan remembers one occasion when going to church wasn't as uplifting as it was meant to be:

When my eldest daughter was three I took her to church on Christmas Eve. It was light when we went and dark when we came out – very dark, because of the blackout; there were no street lights. It was only a little church, so they must have been able to put blackout curtains over the windows. Anyway, we passed a man with a horse and cart delivering fruit and vegetables. The horse had bells on its bridle – to warn you that it was coming, I suppose, because you certainly couldn't see it until you were right up close to it – and my daughter heard the bells and thought it was one of Father Christmas's reindeer. She burst into tears and wept, 'Santa Claus has been and I wasn't in bed!' She thought he'd missed her out. I'd never known her be as willing to go to bed as she was that night.

And Sue, too young to realise what going to church was about, had another not-very-spiritual experience:

My grandmother was very involved in the church and ran the Sunday school. Every year they had a special service with a tableau based round the Christmas crib, and one year – I expect I was three – I was asked… No, I wouldn't have been asked. I was *instructed* to stand by the crib, which was set up between the choir stalls, on the steps by the communion rail. The crib had the Baby Jesus in it (a doll, of course) and then there were adults playing Mary and Joseph and various others who were shepherds and sheep and so on.

There were so few children in the village that there were a lot of adults being big angels, but I was a little angel. I wore a sheet – or it might have been a pillowcase – as my angel's dress and I had a star on my forehead, attached with an elastic band. But it was very rubbery, tight elastic. The primary school teacher was a doughty lady called Agnes Ray; she put my star on for me and it hurt! She told me to be quiet – it was perfectly all right, she said, not hurting at all – but I can still remember how uncomfortable it was. My mother had said to her, 'Sue's a terrible fidget' – which actually I still am, to a certain extent – and she didn't think I'd be able to stand still for any length of time. Miss Ray had said, 'Oh, she'll be all right' and Mum told me later that I was very good: I stood there, this tiny little thing that I was, by the crib, with my hands together as if I were praying, but apparently I got an itch on my nose.

Mum said she watched me, surreptitiously and quite regularly through the service, sneaking my hand up to scratch my nose, then bringing it back to 'prayer position' again. It must have been very funny to watch, but I remember this not at all. I just remember the star and how it hurt.

CHAPTER 10

'THE TROLLEYS WENT ROUND THE WARDS DRAPED WITH STREAMERS'

Another place where people made an effort to make Christmas special was hospital. Not everyone's experience was positive. Barbara was nursing in a London suburb and remembers, 'We decorated the wards and sang carols and that was about it.' But for others it was a surprisingly happy time. One anonymous nurse wrote:

I thought I was unlucky when I found I was to be on duty over Christmas, but I was wrong. It was grand. On Christmas Eve we all got to work with decorations and coloured paper, holly and cotton wool, and in an amazingly short time the whole place was transformed. It really looked like Christmas – and felt like it. The more so when thirty of the nurses went round in a sort of crocodile from ward to ward, with nightlights in makeshift lanterns on poles, singing carols. It was lovely. It made it a real Christmas Eve.

On Christmas Day we were up and had breakfast at the usual time – 7.10 a.m. – but there were eggs and bacon for breakfast. Seven-thirty we were on duty and plenty to do. I was on the maternity ward and we had a busy day there. We had painted in large letters on one of the windows at the top of the ward 'Business as Usual'. And we got what we asked for! Three babies were born. The third arrived just before the King's Speech in the afternoon. I was glad he arrived when he did: I had been looking forward all day to hearing the king speak. The babies were two boys and a girl. The only one to get a Christmassy name was the girl, who was called Carol.

Christmas dinner was the high spot of the day. The honorary surgeon and the physicians came in to carve the turkeys in each ward. Our surgeon, quite a serious, senior gentleman, came dressed as a girl-guide waving a tiny Union Jack – he was incredibly funny. The trolleys went round the wards beautifully decorated and draped with streamers.

One of the most enjoyable features of Christmas was the discarding of the rather rigid formality of a hospital, and finding what human and friendly souls many of the people I'd rather feared really were. It made us feel very like a family – especially with the babies!

Yvonne's patients were not much older. She had left school in the early part of the war and trained as a nurse, then went to work on the children's ward in a south London hospital:

We were very lucky at Lewisham: there was a Canadian organisation that used to send over big boxes of tinned food and stuff that could travel on a boat. The patients – and us – had lots of extra food, which was good for us. Tins of Spam, tins of fruit – all sorts of things that we couldn't get here. They'd even send oranges. Apples they didn't worry about, because we could grow them.

Christmas was lovely on the ward. The children varied in age from a few weeks to ten years old – once they were ten they went on to the adult ward, poor things. A couple of months before Christmas we'd have a little meeting to discuss what we would do and one of the doctors always offered to be Father Christmas. Where he got the costume from, I don't know, but he managed. I suppose he'd had it before the war and just got it out again year after year. He'd go round the ward on Christmas Day and give out presents and laugh and joke with the children.

We hadn't much money, but we used to put together what we had and try to buy a little present for each of the children. Fortunately, at Christmas quite a few of them went home, so there wasn't a tremendous number. But some of them were very ill or chronically ill – polio was the worst thing – so they stayed in. People generally stayed in hospital longer in those days: even if you had your appendix out, today you'd be sent home the next day, but then you didn't get out of bed for a week afterwards.

Some of the parents were very good and used to bring things in, not just for their own child but for the others – they'd ask us to distribute them round the children who didn't have many visitors. And people didn't have much to spare in those days, so it was very kind of them.

The doctors were very good, too: they even arranged entertainment for the children, with proper singers and musicians. We'd get two or three wards together, all those who were able, and have a concert.

We'd do a Christmas dinner and as many of the children as could manage would sit round the table in the middle of the ward. We'd have chicken or whatever we could get – it was lovely. I really enjoyed it on the children's ward. Although it was wartime and there was rationing, we never went hungry, and nor did the patients.

Angela joined the Queen Alexandra's Imperial Military Nursing Service and, at the age of twenty-two, never having been abroad before, she was posted to a hospital at Asansol in West Bengal. Today, this is about 400 kilometres (250 miles) from the border with Bangladesh; in 1942 it was perilously close to the Japanese who had overrun Burma and were setting their sights on India. Angela's patients were more likely to be suffering from malaria than from wounds, however, and Christmas had to go on. She wrote in her diary:

This was the first Christmas away from home for most of our patients and we felt we must make it a good one. There was certainly no problem about the food. Goodies poured in from all directions, particularly from the Red Cross, who were renowned for their tinned fruit cake. Private Watkins, that irrepressible little Geordie, got his pals together and decorated the ward. He had been cured of his bacillary dysentery once but had managed to have another bout of it just before Christmas. I found several of the patients making mistletoe under his direction — little balls of cotton wool stuck on leafy twigs from the compound. Mary, myself and Sister Tuck, who looked very like her namesake Friar Tuck in her girth and rosy complexion, went down to the bazaar on the day before Christmas to buy nuts and dried fruit, then made trifles in the afternoon. Those sisters and doctors who were off duty went to a midnight service and it was 2.30 a.m. when we got to bed.

She goes on to quote from her diary entry for the day itself:

This is one of the happiest Christmas Days I remember. There was a concert on the ward and the St John Ambulance nurses danced with the patients to a band from the RAF units in the area. Captain Murray served the tinned turkey, handing round cans of cold beer to go with it. I think everyone broke their diet today. Private Watkins, a little the worse for drink, chased Matron Tobin down the steps. Everyone sang songs round the piano – 'Tangerine' appears to be the favourite. When the day staff came off duty at 8 p.m. we were swept off to the RAOC mess at Nursa by jeep, but we were all pretty tired and came back here at midnight after singing carols with the men.

CHAPTER 11

'ONLY BULLY BEEF, SPUDS AND BISCUITS'

Those who were on active service marked Christmas as best they could, but the war continued to rage. Despite what Roy in Ealing remembers about the silence of Christmas Eve 1940 in London, there were no real truces – no enemies playing football and singing carols together, as there had been in 1914. A German warship attacked a convoy of merchant shipping in the Atlantic on Christmas Day 1940, and with Japan having entered the war in December 1941 that was a time of fierce conflict in eastern Asia: on Christmas Day the garrison of Hong Kong surrendered after an onslaught lasting nearly three weeks. The airport at Rangoon in Burma was bombed on the same day, as was the Philippine city of San Pablo; the capital Manila suffered the same fate two days later, while in the Mediterranean, Malta endured sixty air raids in Christmas week.

News like this had its inevitable effect on morale back home. Roy recalls:

> Christmas Day that year was very drab. Every aspect of life was grim and I am unable to recall any joyous moment, not even a present of note. Indeed, that very evening it was announced that the British garrison at Hong Kong had been forced to surrender. 'Merry Christmas' was not a popular expression and 'Happy New Year' an even more forlorn hope.

On a more positive note, Germany's eight-month siege of the strategically vital Libyan port of Tobruk was relieved in December 1941, leading Winston Churchill to assert that 'all danger of the Army of the Nile not being able to celebrate Christmas and the New Year in Cairo has been decisively removed'.

But as late as December 1944 and January 1945, when most people in Britain believed that the end of the war was in sight, the Battle of the Bulge was taking place in Belgium, with major assaults on 24 and 25 December, causing heavy American casualties. *Hutchinson's Pictorial History of the War* published two pictures taken that Christmas Day. One shows British troops stealthily crossing a frosty field to approach a farmhouse; the caption remarks that 'there was nothing of a festive character in the task they had to undertake'. In the other image, a soldier sitting alone in a slit trench is eating from a mess tin, with a mug of what is probably tea beside him. 'To provide a seasonal atmosphere,' says the caption, with a touch of desperation, 'he has arranged his greetings cards from home on the edge of the trench.' The poor man may have done his best to make his surroundings festive, but he looks apprehensive and cold.

In other words, for those on active service it was business as usual; for those lucky enough to be in port or on leave there was the chance of some celebration.

The anti-aircraft cruiser *Cairo* was one of many stationed at Loch Ewe in Scotland at the end of 1939, when her crew faced the prospect of Christmas without shore leave. A published 'biography' of *Cairo* and her sister ships recorded their activities:

A concert party had been in rehearsal for some time; news of *Cairo*'s initiative in this field leaked out to Home Fleet ships, isolated, mainly inactive, bored and frustrated. Demands for public shows could not be ignored; a captured German passenger liner became a temporary and expedient Christmas recreation ship, several performances of the pantomime *Woes of Sinbad* were staged to packed houses; audiences came from every ship in Loch Ewe... London's RNVR able seamen as a trio of comely hula-hula girls, Cyril Fisher, William Webb, Joseph Springall, brought the house down at every performance. London sailor volunteers seemed in retrospect, years before their time as 'Drag' artistes; one of the Davies brothers, John, made a specially luscious Princess Lulu, a foil to Marine Corporal Shaw's very ugly and masculine Princess Alure, and the target of delighted shouted obscenities from a celibate all-male audience…

The show was so popular, with so many demands for repeat performances on individual vessels, that *Cairo* had to wait until New Year's Eve for her own show. A year later, she was on a 'winter-gloomed Tyne', while her sister ships *Calcutta* and *Coventry* were in Egypt, celebrating Christmas by playing rugby against an RAF team and visiting the 'fleshpots of Alexandria'. Then in 1941 *Coventry* was in India, where some of her men received 'hospitality in almost overwhelming quantity and variety':

> British, Indian and Anglo Indian families took in men from the ship and Calabar camp for Christmas celebrations. They received invitations to all special seasonal sporting events, balls and dances. The scale of hospitality extended to unrestricted loans of yachts by owner members of the Bombay Yacht club, something that received enthusiastic acceptance by the wardroom; several short cruises, crewed by mixed parties of officers and ratings, were organised by and led by Donald Peyton Jones, the irrepressible Captain Royal Marines.

This jollification was in sharp contrast to the news received from Britain describing hardships, air raids and casualties; it also didn't alter the fact that this was the third Christmas in a row that *Coventry*'s men had been away from home. Nor were they blind to the contrast between the life they were briefly living and 'the horrendous squalor and starving poverty that was the hopeless lot of teeming millions' living on the streets of Bombay and other Indian cities.

Robert Stanford Tuck was one of the RAF's most distinguished fighter pilots; by December 1940 he was a squadron leader and he and his squadron of Hurricanes were stationed at RAF Coltishall in Norfolk:

> All morning the Coltishall squadrons were at readiness and in the afternoon they flew some abortive patrols. And in the evening the service tradition of the officers and N.C.O.s waiting upon the men at dinner table was observed as usual – and then of course there was a general beer-up in which rank was eliminated and the airmen exchanged tunics with the pilots. L.A.C. Hillman made a weird Cinderella, having made his swop with the C.O. – Tuck's tunic came down halfway to his knees, but it couldn't be buttoned across the Cockney's bulky chest.

The Royal Navy destroyer HMS *Jervis* became famous for her charmed life, seeing much action without losing a single member of her crew. This luck extended to spending most wartime Christmases in port. (In many accounts from other ships, Christmas passes without a mention, as ships were mid-battle, in convoy or engaged in training.) In this record, her captain, Philip Mack, is also referred to as Captain (D) – designate – of the 7th Flotilla, of which *Jervis* was a part. The first Christmas of the war, based at Immingham in

Lincolnshire, was described as 'a low key and sombre affair, full of uncertainties about the future'. In 1940, however, *Jervis* was in the Mediterranean and enjoying 'the remarkable good fortune to be in harbour on Christmas Day':

The messdecks had been decorated with bunting and signal flags borrowed from Chief Yeoman Harris and his signal department, and some individual messes, with considerable imagination and ingenuity, had been converted into colourful grottoes. The mess caterers and cooks had succeeded in converting the 'pusser's' issue of pork and rather stringy chickens (obtained from the canteen manager) into palatable seasonal dishes, and some messes found ingredients which – liberally laced with illegally hoarded rum issues – became lethal Christmas pudding substitutes. Aft, the wardroom staff excelled themselves: 'The Maltese staff competed wonderfully and turned the wardroom into a cross between an early Victorian conservatory, the harvest thanksgiving and the village on a carnival night.'

Philip Mack gave further indications of his stamina – he toured the messdecks at 10:00 immediately after an earlier than usual 'tot' issue; he exchanged good humoured and affectionate banter at every junior mess, and accepted innumerable 'sippers'. At 10:30 he entertained the chief and petty officers in the wardroom with his staff and ship's officers, then at 11:30 he hosted a reception for the flotilla captains and their officers, finally sitting down at the head of the wardroom table at 14:45 to commence Christmas lunch with his own officers. Throughout this social marathon Captain Mack's reputation as a raconteur and host became even more firmly established.

The following year, in dry dock in Alexandria, Captain Mack did the same social rounds, then joined the wardroom in a 'hilarious game of charades'; he was doing his impression of a German Tiger tank, disguised in a cardboard costume, when his commander-in-chief paid an unexpected visit, an intrusion with which he dealt with his usual panache.

But even for 'lucky *Jervis*', the good fortune of being able to celebrate Christmas couldn't last. In 1942 she was involved in the Siege of Malta; by Christmas, supplies were running very short and one of her crew recorded, 'This is the worst Christmas of my life – no beer, no grub, only bully beef [canned corned beef], spuds and biscuits – and everyone is chocker [fed up].'

Dan was with the Royal Horse Artillery in North Africa for Christmas 1942, and seems to have managed some fun and games:

Although we worked hard we played hard as well, and got up to all sorts of things to keep everybody amused. We held race meetings and dog shows (the pye-dogs we found had to be seen to be believed). We used to go duck shooting with .303 rifles but didn't have much luck. Once I did shoot what I thought was some sort of goose and gave it to the Mess Sergeant for Christmas. The flesh turned out black and proved to be a buzzard. We spent Christmas at Tmimi [Libya] and of course this is the occasion when officers are entertained by sergeants. I remember one of my sergeants, Stud Groom, mixing a noxious drink of whisky, gin and crème de menthe in a half pint glass and giving it to Colonel Douglas Darling of the Rifle Brigade, who drank it and then said, 'That's nice, I'll have another one of these.' He may have passed out on his return to his tent, but he became a bit of a folk hero to our sergeants.

Two years later, having taken part in the Battle of Arnhem ('all I can remember was the mud and the rain'), Dan's regiment was with the King's Royal Rifle Corps in the Netherlands:

Christmas was spent with the KRRC holding a large stretch of the west bank of the River Maas. It was a ticklish situation there because we were very thin on the ground and opposite us was the very aggressive German parachute division. On Christmas night I was with a signaller at an observation post with the riflemen. It was snowing, it was bitterly cold and I was thoroughly browned off because I could hear the Germans happily singing 'Silent Night' across the river and I knew that RHQ would be having some sort of party as well. I cheered myself up, however, by sending them a signal saying that three men in black uniforms with silver SS badges had come across the river in rubber boats and had asked where RHQ was, so I told them. Was this OK?

Alec was in the Fleet Air Arm and had two very different experiences of Christmas:

> I joined up in December 1942 and spent my first weeks at the base at Lee-on-Solent. All I remember about that Christmas is having a terrible cold, almost flu, and my feet playing up because of the uncomfortable boots we'd all been issued. I was very sorry for myself and wondering what I'd volunteered for.
>
> The following year it was very different. I'd done six months' training in Trinidad and was heading back to the UK via New York. I spent Christmas in Brooklyn Barracks and had a wonderful time. There were none of the shortages we'd got used to at home and we went skating in that area they flooded in Times Square. The English-Speaking Union was also based there and we got lots of free tickets for shows. It was very pleasant after the austerity of the UK.

Aldwyn had joined the RAF and he too had contrasting experiences of Christmas. December 1942 found him at RAF Credenhill, near Hereford:

> I was on a training course for the care and maintenance of torpedoes. I don't know if you've ever thought much about a torpedo, but it is quite a complicated piece of mechanism. It has its own little engine and a server motor that gives power to the rudders that guide it. Then there's a depth-gear that controls the depth at

which it settles when it drops... So there's quite a lot to it, and it took about two and a half months' training to learn all about maintaining and repairing it. This was important because for training purposes the same torpedoes were used over and over again. If you are going to use a torpedo in anger, as it were, you put an explosive warhead on it. You fire it and it blows up and that is that. But for an exercise you use the same body and put a training head on it, which is full of water rather than explosive. When it lands on a target, the water is expelled and the torpedo bobs back to the surface. It is recovered, brought back to the workshops and serviced, just as a car might be serviced. Then it has another training head screwed on so that it's ready to be used again.

All of which is a long way of saying that Christmas 1942 more or less passed me by, because I was learning to service torpedoes. We had a good Christmas meal, I'm sure, and I joined in what conviviality there was. I was perhaps drinking tea when everyone else was drinking beer, but the company was good and I was quite happy.

1943-4 saw a complete change of scene:

In 1943 I had the good fortune to be posted to Ceylon (now Sri Lanka), the 'Pearl of the Indian Ocean'. I don't suppose our Christmas was very different from the way it would have been on any other RAF station. The cooks made a special effort to provide a Christmas meal, primarily from dried or tinned ingredients but still, one might say, sumptuous when compared to the rather basic, bland and unadventurous daily rations. I was in a place called Ratmalana, just a few miles from Colombo, the capital, in a special torpedo unit that was meant to move on to some remote island in the Pacific. This island would have a runway and some torpedo bombers and the plan was that we would attack the Japanese fleet from there. But it just didn't happen. Why? Goodness knows. In the Forces your life isn't your own – you do what you're told to do and go where you're told to go. So I didn't go to the Pacific. I stayed in Ceylon and carried on servicing torpedoes.

The following December I was sent to Koggala, another RAF station in Ceylon, where they had flying boats whose job was to drop depth charges and mines and so on in the Indian Ocean. I and one other colleague from Ratmalana were to do the maintenance for them. I was a bit put out that I had to leave my friends just before Christmas, but, as I say, we did as we were told. When we arrived at Koggala we had to go through the usual drill – see the doctor, see the dentist, see the equipment people and make sure our gear was in order – and then we were told to get lost for a few days. This was I think Saturday; Christmas was Monday and they didn't want us to report until the Tuesday. So we did as we were told and got lost. While we were with the doctor we had heard that there was an ambulance going into Colombo, so we arranged to travel with that; then we took a local bus and turned up back at Ratmalana on Christmas Eve.

I still have my diary from that period, and I wrote that there was quite a party in the NAAFI that night and I was persuaded to have a taste of alcohol for the first time in my life. Somehow or other they'd managed to get hold of all sorts of different things – crème de mocha, whisky, vermouth, port – but I didn't have very much. At eleven o'clock I got a lift in a lorry to Christ Church, Galle Face, which was the cathedral for Colombo, for a 'watch-night' service. On Christmas morning I've noted a slap-up breakfast; then gathering in the cookhouse at two o'clock for a very good Christmas dinner served by the officers and senior NCOs: turkey, pork, vegetables, Christmas pudding, coffee, chocolate biscuits, plus a gift of a hundred cigarettes and a bottle of beer, which I promptly gave away.

It's interesting to look back and see that, despite the fact we were in Ceylon, we were eating the same sort of rations we'd have had anywhere else. The one concession I remember to Singhalese food is that we had fresh fruit – pineapple, apricots I think, and certainly cashew nuts. One of the great luxuries was when we used to go across the camp to one of the hangars that had been converted into a cinema. The local staff would be there, with piles of pineapples and sharp knives. They would hold the pineapple by its stalk, cut the top off, trim the sides, then cut it into four – so we'd have a quarter of a pineapple to take into the cinema with us instead of popcorn! That was quite a delicacy – I'd had tinned pineapple before, but never fresh.

Ivan was in the RAF, stationed at Number 4 Radio School Madley, Herefordshire:

I had a very lucky escape in Christmas 1944 – one of many I've had in my life. I'd been married in the September and one weekend in the late autumn I was overcome by a desire to see my wife, so I went home without leave. As a result I was put in the air-crew glasshouse for three weeks.

During that time the crew I should have been with was assigned to do a training flight and they had to take another wireless operator, because of my being in the glasshouse. When they came back to land at Swinderby in Lincolnshire, they were told, 'We're changing runways, go round for half an hour and then come back.' So they did, and were never heard of again. No one really knows what happened, but it was assumed that they were shot down by one of the Junkers 88s that used to creep in over the Wash at that time. Having gone AWOL saved my life.

Despite this tragedy, normal training work had to go on. As did the Christmas celebrations a few days later:

I've kept the menu from our Christmas dinner. It shows that we were being well looked after: roast turkey and roast pork, sage and onion stuffing, apple sauce, roast and creamed potatoes, Brussels sprouts and peas, followed by Christmas pudding, mince pies, custard sauce and dessert apples. Then there were biscuits, cheese and nuts, beer, minerals and cigarettes.

We didn't put on any entertainment, but we had a piano in the mess and we sang our usual RAF songs – not all of them suitable for mixed company.

Over Christmas 1944 Lucy was stationed in Rome with Allied Forces Headquarters, which controlled Allied operations in the Mediterranean. ('Postman's Knock', mentioned in this anecdote, is a party game that involves a lot of kissing and tends to be popular towards the end of a convivial evening.)

Decorating the ante-room was of course quite a job, but we managed to make it look quite attractive. The troops had their Christmas dinner there, as it was the largest room in the building, their canteen being too small to accommodate everyone at once. Two or three AT officers cooked the mess breakfast on Christmas Day, and I thoroughly enjoyed this. All the batmen came and had tea and chatted, and the atmosphere became cheery very early in the proceedings. After breakfast there was a fancy dress football match, for which various articles of feminine attire were begged and borrowed from the ATS. It was very funny, and I believe 'Doc' went as Julius Caesar. The dinner was a great success, and accompanied by the usual greetings, the band playing, and the evergreen sprigs of mistletoe in evidence. The officers of course did the waiting. There was an all ranks dance that evening in the village, to which most of us repaired for a time, and where an inordinate amount of white wine and vermouth was consumed, and a thoroughly good time was had by all…

Tony and I planned to give a party for the ATS girls. It would be as homely as possible, and to this end we had decided to find somewhere in Rome where it could be held at reasonable expense. We hunted high and low without success, and finally almost in despair we asked the porter at the Eden Hotel and he suggested the Pensione Giulio. So off we went, and I had to do the translating, for the two little old ladies who ushered us in, the Signorine Giulio, owners of the Pensione, spoke very little English and Tony very little Italian. However, they received us with old-world courtesy, agreed to lay on a supper for us, and showed us two rooms which we could use. We arranged the menu and on the day itself took small presents and decorations along. The male end was composed of Tony, and a few sergeants and corporals from the office staff. Altogether there were about a dozen of us. The affair was a great success, thanks largely to the Signorine, who cooked us a magnificent meal, including spaghetti with tomato sauce, roast chicken and tinned Christmas pudding, which we took along and showed them how to heat. They provided suitable wine, and with great charm and real kindliness made us welcome and at home. Afterwards various games were played, some for prizes, but the favourite among the girls seemed to be forfeits, and towards the end 'Postman's Knock' was mooted; fortunately it was time to depart, for their passes expired at midnight.

This party was such a success that another was organised later in the winter. This time the girls made time for 'Postman's Knock'.

Margaret was a nurse in India, and also had a merry Christmas in 1944. Returning to her unit after a long period of leave, she discovered that they had orders to be ready to move by the midnight train. The train didn't in fact leave until 4 a.m., when the unit was sent out of the jungle to Dibrugarh, in the eastern part of Assam, for Christmas:

We had a wonderful party – tinned milk mixed with gin and whisky, which was rechristened tiger's milk. I remember someone falling into a rain-filled slit trench, holding aloft a Christmas cake and a bottle of Scotch. How the unit escaped a court marshal was a miracle.

But all this merry-making was the exception rather than the rule. For most people in the services, Christmas brought the usual wartime combination of monotony, loneliness, shortages and fear.

Eric, a twenty-one-year-old journalist at the start of the war, joined up immediately. With what he described as extraordinary ease, he became part of the Royal Army Service

Corps in Aldershot, where 'boredom and deprivation were instant'. By December 1939 he was in France:

> The next day the whole company, complete with camouflaged petrol tankers and other ancillary vehicles, set off for the village of Beaumont-sur-Sarthe. Here we spent Christmas, queuing for meals over an overflowing, squelching cesspit which was emptied by the French authorities in the second week. There was virtually no blackout in Beaumont, and when we paraded in the village square we were photographed by the local weekly, which duly provided any German interested with news of our arrival.

In November 1940, the SS *Automedon* was sunk by a German surface raider. After a month its survivors were transferred to a captured Norwegian tanker called *Storstad*, which was serving as a prison ship. Some years later, Captain S W Roskill published his account of the experience:

> She already had on board men from eight other sunk or captured ships. The *Storstad* then passed some 600 miles south of the Cape of Good Hope, in which latitude the prisoners found the cold extremely trying. So passed Christmas Day, 1940. To celebrate it their captors issued a bottle of beer to each man: but no extra rations were served out. However, the British officers were touched to receive, at the Chinese New Year, a message from the *Automedon*'s No. 2 Chinese 'in which he said how sorry

243

he was for our people, and that although our bodies were troubled we must not let our minds be troubled' – a very apposite piece of oriental philosophy to address to prisoners-of-war.

Attached to the 1/1st Gurkha Rifles in Iran and Iraq, Lieutenant B F Spiller spent Christmas 1941 in Basra. Billeted in the Shatt-el-Arab hotel, which doubled as a brothel, he didn't relish the experience, recording:

I don't remember enjoying Christmas since I was a child. This Christmas Day was the worst ever. A small but virulent 'Baghdad boil' on my cheek elected to burst in the afternoon. I took to my bed and tried to sleep. The racket made rest impossible. All around was pandemonium: doors slamming, corks popping, bells ringing without being answered, hotel staff arguing, demoniac laughter echoing down the corridors. In the evening I tried to drown the pain with aspirin and went out to watch couples with glazed expressions shunting round a dance floor. Several people got drunk and were quietly removed. Returning to the Shatt-el-Arab, I found that the signs of festivity had increased. A fire-extinguisher had been let off, flooding the hall; and in the courtyard a trio of sodden soldiers were leaning into the fountain, trying to catch the carp. Upstairs there was a scene of devastation. A bunch of drunken soldiers had broken into bedrooms, announcing that they were military police. Their behaviour suggested a demolition gang. My room was untouched, although those opposite and on both sides had been ransacked.

Sikander, the little Chaldean Christian room-boy, told me that two soldiers had knocked down a genuine military policeman and kicked him on the head. He had been distressed to see British soldiers fighting among themselves. 'S'ils se battraient avec les arabes ce serait bien *[if they fought with the Arabs, that would be fine].*'

Two days later, Lieutenant Spiller wrote to his wife:

My life continues on the same even pattern of long office hours, interesting enough work and sometimes a quiet bar crawl in the evening. It is discreet because of the price of drink. Actually there is a very good system of rationed whisky whereby an officer like me who doesn't live in a mess can buy a bottle of whisky on the cheap from the NAAFI if he gets there in time. A colonel told me that he always bought chocolate and found it an excellent substitute for whisky in the cold weather, but I have not had the same experience.

There were turkeys for dinner at Christmas here, which I suppose there weren't at home. They were so badly cooked that there was practically no taste in them. All meat out here is pretty dull eating, because there is no proper feeding for the animals when they are alive. I don't recommend Iraq as a holiday resort.

At seventeen Richard lied about his age in order to join the Queen's Own Royal West Kent Regiment. Having become a wireless operator and still only twenty-one, he was in Italy for Christmas 1943. A corporal in his unit was killed and one of the officers had his lower leg blown off by one of their own mines. The officer had to undergo a further amputation on a makeshift bench, with a saw borrowed from one of the locals and minimal anaesthetic. Rations were getting very low and, to make matters worse, it started to snow:

> None of us had ever seen anything like it. It started one afternoon and, by the following morning, it was three feet deep.
>
> I was only using my wireless at 9 o'clock in the morning and at 3 o'clock in the afternoon. I explained to base that we were going on to quarter rations. They said they had been in touch with the RAF and a Dakota aircraft would be dropping rations by parachutes. We all looked and cheered when it came in sight. We saw the chutes open but, alas, they drifted down to the bottom of the valley. The Germans must have been highly delighted. They had ski troops and we watched as they gathered our rations. We could do nothing to stop them.
>
> It started to snow again. It was a couple of days to Christmas. I explained all that had happened to base. Evidently another drop was to take place but, every transmission for two days, they said the weather was too bad for flying. We knew that ourselves as, by now, the snow was fifteen feet deep. It had all drifted our way. Things were getting desperate now. Christmas Day we had half a cup of weak tea with three hard biscuits

for breakfast. For dinner we had a tin of corned beef between six of us, plus a slice of tinned peach. Later, we had another half cup of tea with a couple of biscuits. We were told we would have our Christmas when we were relieved. What happened? We never had it.

Some of our lads had made tunnels through the snow. Everyone was coming to me to ask for a sheet of my message pad. When their bowels worked, which was not often, they threw the result out over the snow.

At last, the sun shone. We were told to make a letter L with gas capes on the snow, in the centre of our position. Another drop had been arranged. Oh, what a day! First of all, two fighter planes came and strafed the German side of the valley. Then another one came, escorting the Dakotas and strafing the enemy positions. The Dakotas came in very low, right over our heads. The baskets dropped right on the gas capes. It was wonderful – and the fighter planes waggled their wings as they went back. The food baskets were well-packed: everything that was needed, even cigarettes for everyone. We all had a decent meal at last.

After his stint in France quoted earlier, Eric was posted to Lagos, where he edited 'News from Nigeria', a fortnightly bulletin for West African troops fighting in Burma. He also wrote and read scripts on Nigerian radio, one of which described Christmas Day 1944. Akyab [now Sittwe], a crucial port and supply base, had been in Japanese hands for two years:

First of all, if you've got your atlas handy, get it out, turn to Burma, and put your finger on – AKYAB. Now let your eye travel north to RATHEDAUNG. For Rathedaung, where the West Africans fought with British and Indian Forces, fell after a successful Christmas week's fighting. A successful week not only in this sector of the Arakan, but on all the Burma fronts.

Even in this grim war theatre where Nature and the Japanese are the foes, Christmas was observed and British, American and Empire airmen acted as flying Santa Claus. Flying over areas which a few weeks ago were the scenes of bitter fighting, they dropped Christmas presents – parcels from home, fresh meat, poultry, fruit drinks, and a lot of other delicacies which we like to eat at Christmas time.

But the most popular were the 'Turkey Specials' – bombers which flew 11,000 pounds of turkeys to troops in the forward areas.

Other pilots had grimmer tasks to carry out, and less appropriate to the season. For example, there was the Squadron Leader who shot out of the skies two of the four Japanese bombers on a Christmas night raid on Bengal. And the other two were damaged also.

The West Africans were close behind the 25th Indian Division, when they reached the tip of the Mayu Peninsula which narrows to a finger of land pointing at Akyab, four miles away across a rocky channel.

It was on Christmas Day that troops of the 15th Corps reached Foul Point, on the Mayu River Estuary.

They had made a lightning advance from Maungdaw, and they were full of fight.

Now they stood opposite Akyab, Burma's fifth town in population, and the supply base for the Japanese who were going to conquer India.

It was at this stage that the bombers took a hand. Massed fleets of Allied bombers came flying in to deliver the fiercest air blow yet dealt in the South-East Asia Command. They swept the road from Akyab up to Kyawktaw, still in the Kaladan, with bombs and machine gun fire. Off the roads went the Jap supply columns, and pilots returning were able to report: the Japs are on the run; they're pulling out of Akyab.

It was the old story of air superiority – almost air monopoly, and the first big victory of the Burma war was close at hand.

The men of the 15th Corps didn't want to waste any time. They gathered together a mixed fleet composed of all the shipping and small warships they could get hold of, and made the four-mile crossing to Akyab with guns and tanks, and highly trained commando troops. But when they got there, they found the Japs had fled.

And so Akyab fell. Its fate had been sealed on Christmas Day when the men of the 15th Corps reached Foul Point. Akyab is a prize indeed, with its harbour which can take cruisers up to 10,000 tons, and its all-weather airfield and seven smaller landing grounds. Our ships can now bring supplies direct from India to Akyab, which dominates also the inland waterways which will now become our vital supply.

In 1944 Tom was with the Eighth Army in an unspecified part of North Africa or the Middle East. On New Year's Eve even the thought that the war would soon be over failed to cheer him. He wrote to his wife Betty, who was serving in the WRNS.

New Year's Eve about twenty-one hundred hours – shades of New Years of days gone by – I am in the office truck. I have just put my bed down, having come in for a few minutes to relieve the guard. I am sleeping in this truck at the moment whilst the other sergeant is away on leave at a rest camp. He should have been back tonight but he's probably snowed up somewhere.

I have a glass of vermouth with me, we have just managed to make our capture last the distance, tonight will see the end of it. Already the first 'Auld Lang Syne' has been sung. Somehow, though, I don't feel particularly cheerful, tomorrow the start of a new year and what a prospect. I admit that as far as I'm concerned it will mean that unless I get in the way of a stray shell or bomb I will return home, that is a lovely thought, but the general situation fills me with considerable foreboding.

Tomorrow sees the end of my fourth year abroad & the day after that the start of my fifth. After I have written this I have to go and drink with my friend the 'Goat', a very pleasant gentleman with whom I came abroad. He is also in a dark mood, in fact it is rather peculiar but all but the latest arrivals are in such a mood today. Don't know why, maybe we are a bit tired. It may be that we think that though we will return home next year we will be away again before Christmas. Still it's not right to write in that strain. I beg your pardon. There's no end to it!

How nice it would be if we were dressed in our best 'come hither' outfits, casting a roving eye around the place, perhaps having a 'small one' just to please somebody and then shaking a nimble hip. Maybe a party afterwards, or just ham and eggs in that place in Mosley St.

I have some doubts whether my 'soup and fish' [evening dress] *would fit now as I have increased my girth slightly* [...] *Hair much greyer and face more lined – definitely a hoary old bachelor. Yes, I think so, though the twinkle would be there if opportunity provided the chance.*

That's the lot for this year. A poor letter, I'm afraid – very sorry. I will now drink your health.

Cheers and may we both be out of the services by this time in 1945.

CHAPTER 12

'THE BEST CHRISTMAS SO FAR IN PRISON'

Accounts of the horrors suffered by long-term prisoners of war abound: one woman described an uncle who had been in the Hong Kong police and was 6 feet 5 inches (1.96 metres) tall; when he returned from several years' internment he weighed 5 stone (32 kilograms) and died within a year. Similar stories could be told of thousands upon thousands of others.

What is perhaps less well documented is the sheer mind-numbing boredom, discomfort and despair felt by prisoners who had no idea when or if they were ever going to be released, or what was happening to people at home. Latrines shared with dozens of others were only the most obvious cause for complaint. Most prisoners had been captured with the clothes they stood up in and little else. The 1929 Geneva Convention on the treatment of prisoners of war obliged the detaining power to provide clothing, including underwear and shoes, but it was not until some years into the war that the British and Commonwealth governments decided to supply those of their forces who had been taken prisoner with a change of uniform. The thought was that pictures of well-turned-out prisoners would be good for the morale of those who saw them back home.

In the meantime, the Joint War Organisation of the British Red Cross Society and the Order of St John had been sending food parcels to prison camps overseas. At the rate of one parcel per man per week, this peaked at about 163,000 parcels per week and amounted to 20 million in the course of the war. Friends and relatives could also send a limited number of packages, supplying their loved ones with such basics as socks and underwear.

Special Red Cross packages for Christmas were despatched in August to POW camps in Germany and Italy, with each 1944 parcel containing:

8oz tin baked beans
8oz tin butter
4oz packet chocolate
2oz packet custard powder
8oz tin honey
14oz tin condensed milk
6½oz packet pancake batter
16oz tin pork and stuffing
3½oz tin sardines
12oz tin Spam

16oz tin stewed steak
4oz bar sugar
20oz packet tea
16oz tin Christmas cake
16oz tin Christmas pudding

[1 ounce equates to a little over 28 grams]

In addition, each prisoner was sent a separate package containing a hundred cigarettes. Those imprisoned in Germany received a Christmas card in their parcels. The Italian government did not permit this; its counter-proposal that the War Organisation could distribute cards that had been printed in Italy was refused, on the not unreasonable grounds that it would have meant putting money into the hands of the enemy.

As the German infrastructure began to collapse after the D-Day landings of June 1944, fewer Red Cross parcels got through: Christmas 1944, with the end of the war in Europe in sight, was one of the most miserable and malnourished for prisoners. It was also perishingly cold, as this Australian account from the notorious Colditz Castle records:

Christmas Day of 1944 began as an uninvitingly frosty morning. The temperature was 12°F – 20° below freezing point.

We celebrated by digging into our meagre rations, and breakfasted on a large helping of porridge, some scrambled eggs, coffee, toast and marmalade, and then attended Padre Platt's morning service.

Lunch, or rather dinner, was served successively to various floors; pea soup and bacon, roast veal, pork, mashed potatoes and peas. We each received a large ration of this, but it would have been more enjoyable had it been a little warmer than tepid! We made our own supper of toast and marmalade, and enjoyed some marvellous (and hot!) tinned Christmas pudding. We toasted what must surely be our last Christmas in captivity.

On Boxing Day Johnny Rawson organised a mammoth whist drive, with some chocolate as first prize. It was a fine contest, finally won by Major Victor Campbell. At 5.30 that evening we attended the Christmas pantomime, 'Hey Diddle Snow White'... It was great fun, with a Wicked Duke, Good and Bad Fairies, Prince Charming, Gangster Bodyguards and Japanese Torturers!...

The new year – 1945 – was heralded in on a cold note, and the fact it had started merely compounded our misery. There was very little coal for heating, and the only good news was that on 3 January we were issued three Red Cross parcels per five persons.

Nazi propaganda would have you believe that it was impossible to escape from Colditz, but the claim merely encouraged the castle's more enterprising prisoners to try harder. The sixteen Brits who were there for Christmas 1940 had celebrated by starting work on a plan to dig their way out via the sewer tunnels. It kept them busy until the proposed escape date at the end of May 1941, when they were foiled by the German sentry, whom they had bribed to turn a blind eye, giving them away to the prison Kommandant.

David had been chaplain at Eton College and saw a mere fifteen days of active service with the British Expeditionary Force in France before being captured. He spent five Christmases in captivity in Poland; the third, in 1942, seems to have been quite a cheerful occasion, largely thanks to the effort he had put into rehearsing his makeshift choir:

Everybody was in tremendously good form here. The Christmas show ended on Wednesday night and I had my Service of Lessons and Carols on Christmas Eve, well attended. Choir and soloists repaid all my work a thousandfold by singing better than ever before. Nice services here on Christmas Day, and at the hospital, and came back in time for our evening meal, which flattened me in traditional style. All credit to the Red Cross who got the Christmas parcels here, plus plum puddings and all. Various 'itinerant' concert parties in the Fort, one of which, complete with piano and band, arrived en bloc in our room and played to us even when we had gone to bed. The Polish officer, whom we call Felix, dreamt that he was sitting in front of an enormous pudding, while I, dressed in the uniform of the local police, was standing over him and insisting with dire threats that he finish it. It was the best Christmas so far in prison, and I think everyone had a good time… On Boxing Day we had our annual officers' gathering at another camp, saw the Stalag Art and Crafts Exhibition, at soccer England drew with Scotland, and more over-eating. In spite of our preoccupations I know that everybody was thinking of home, and many men were saying to me that they hoped that their wives and children were having as good a Christmas, and wished that you all knew what a great time everyone here was having. The family spirit was wonderful…

1943 was rather more sombre, as it brought the news of the death in a mental hospital of a young man David had known in prison. As chaplain, he took a long and tedious journey to conduct the funeral service, only to find when he arrived that it had already taken place:

I had to see the asylum authorities about Alan's effects, and while we waited for various formalities to be completed, I had some talk with a Polish male nurse, who told me something of the appalling conditions in the hospital. Food, he said, was in very short supply, and I noticed in the register that I had to sign that there was a death rate of three to five inmates daily.

In 1944, David was invited to the concentration camp at Graudenz to conduct a service on Christmas Day. On arrival with an interpreter called Braun, he was told by the Kommandant that he would not be permitted to talk privately to any of the men:

'On a previous visit,' I said, 'I was allowed by your predecessor to talk to the men under supervision.'

'*Nein*,' he replied, '*dass ist verboten.*'

'But,' I said, 'would it be possible to make arrangements with the Senior British Officer or Warrant Officer to allow those who wish to join in Holy Communion after the service?'

'*Abendmahl ist von Berlin streng verboten*,' ('Communion is strictly forbidden by Berlin') he replied, and of this strange interdiction clearly no more could be said.

'May I visit the men in hospital?' I asked.

'*Nein, dass ist auch verboten.*'

The next objection was to the hymn sheets and carols that David removed from his case:

Braun picked one up and handed it to him.

'But they have no censor stamp on them,' he exclaimed.

Braun and I tried to explain to him that they were Christian hymns and carols, sent to us from Geneva by the International YMCA with OKW [Oberkommando der Wehrmacht – High Command of the Armed Forces] permission and were used in all POW camps. After some argument he asked for a translation, and I watched as a curious look of perplexity spread over his face. Braun had mischievously chosen to translate 'Now thank we all our God' '*Nun danket…*'

'*Dass ist Deutsches Hymnus*,' ('That is a German hymn') he exclaimed.

The point was made, and we set off for the chapel escorted by his interviewer.

The service over, David and Braun proceeded to another camp, where they were served Christmas dinner by an 'ebullient' corporal named Williams:

> …A real Christmas dinner with two large black market chickens with all the trimmings. Braun was not the man to resist or query such temptation, and enjoyed it as much as we did. He was the last to realise what was happening when the tell-tale remains on our plates were hurriedly swept from under our noses and shovelled into the stove. News had reached Williams that a strange German officer had been spotted heading for our room. Williams was already awaiting a court-martial for illegal trading with the civilian population.

Eric was a British military chaplain captured by the Japanese after the fall of Singapore, and imprisoned there – along with some 50,000 others – in the Changi Prison Complex. During his three and a half years as a prisoner of war, including a year on the notorious Burma Railway, he secretly kept a detailed diary – and sketches, maps, orders of service and other memorabilia – which came to light only after his wife's death in 2011. Writing that he regarded his imprisonment as 'the most wonderful opportunity' for a chaplain, he set about converting an abandoned mosque within the prison complex into a church, which he named St George's, and encouraged his fellow prisoners to make use of it. This is part of his description of Christmas 1942, his first as a POW:

On Christmas Eve the moon made the whole landscape of tall clustered palms and squat huts swim in a warm light. That moon is not the pale thing of the north but is as masterful as the sun itself. Below the dome of St. George's the atap-roofed verandahs twinkled with hanging lamps made from half shells of cocoanuts [sic] and inside a bully beef tin filled with palm oil and having a floating wick. Then nearer still at the entrance stood a Christmas tree, a local imitation of our English fir reaching to the roof. Reflecting the lights from little lamps fastened to the branches were stars, small horse-shoes, all shapes and sizes of tinfoil covered objects. Then inside the church itself, the pillars were covered with ferns, and along the low wall between the arches stood pots of coloured flowers. Both Dutch and British troops went out with trucks to collect all these decorations. But one's gaze was centred on the chancel, here in a mass of candle light, the Altar was emphasised as the focal point. A row of candles were fastened above the Altar, and three-branched tall candlesticks stood on either side; the flowers and feathery green ferns enhanced the setting for the Celebration of Holy Communion that was to take place at midnight.

As a Church of England chaplain, Eric was particularly moved by the enthusiasm with which other denominations greeted his plans: eight hundred men packed into and around St George's for the Midnight Eucharist on Christmas Eve. He also praised the performance given by the prison choir and orchestra, many of whose members were professionals.

But perhaps the most touching part of his account concerns 'the brainwave and grand idea' that someone had of 'making toys for the sixty British children in the civilian jail which is situated just outside the perimeter wire of our camp' – children who for one reason or another had not been evacuated from Singapore before it surrendered:

A week before Christmas an exhibition of toys was arranged; to visit it was to recapture the scene of the toy department of any large London store. It was thrilling, scooters, engines, prams, rocking horses, and smaller toys such as dolls and whipping tops, they were all beautifully made and finished. The rapt expression on men's faces as they lingered over this display, was a foretaste of the thrill that those kiddies must have had in receiving each four or five of these toys. The Japanese authorities gave permission for these toys to be sent to the jail, and a touching letter of thanks was received from the women's representative in the prison. It would have been marvellous to have been present, though it is not difficult to picture that scene. It must have done much to brighten the life of those little children.

All this was in advance of Christmas Day itself, which began with a church service, in the dark, at half-past seven in the morning:

...the chancel with its many candles reflected light sufficient until the coming of the dawn, and so followed another service and then breakfast. During the meal the orchestra grouped on the centre of the padang [playing field] played carols. Our meals throughout the day were most attractive. For the first time we were able to drink coffee with tinned milk, a luxury, and breakfast was made more exciting by some fish fried with chipped potatoes. A Sung Eucharist followed by a Carol Service completed the services for the day. In the evening we ate a most superior dinner. Ten scraggy cockerels carefully nursed for months provided the 'plat du jour', preceded by soup and followed by a fair imitation of plum pudding. It was the right colour and had dates in it. We drank a home-brewed pineapple cyder, though the word 'cyder' makes it sound more potent than it really was, but in the hackneyed words of those local newspaper reports – 'a good time was had by all'. A gigantic concert on the padang filled the evening and at eleven o'clock we joined the Dutch Officers for some supper. A subscription to the value of tenpence was raised, and in a mess room decorated with paper tablecloths and lit by little lamps seventy officers were seated round a horseshoe-shaped table. A three-course meal began with a thick soup, a speciality of Java, then a sardine sandwich. This was the first slice of bread tasted

263

for many months, for the supply of flour was exhausted some time ago. The sweet may best be described as a sweet soup, a favourite from the East Indies, called Kolak, which was rich and sweet and pleasant and seemed to contain pineapple and cocoanut juice. Speeches and toast were made and the day was rounded off with coffee sometime in the small hours.

Eric concludes his account with a further reflection on his pastoral role:

I was surprised but thrilled that so many made a real effort to prepare for Christmas by asking that their confessions might be heard. It was more than the usual few instructed folk to whom this was their custom. Quite a few men, even including Dutch, came to me in Church for this purpose before the festival. I feel I can look back on those days as a definite milestone in my life.

Atholl was another who kept a secret record of his time in captivity. A young Scottish soldier captured by the Japanese in 1942, he smuggled his diaries out at the end of the war and apparently didn't look at them for twenty years or more. He describes the day-to-day boredom and hardships, the poor food and frequent attacks of 'the squitters'. There is even one chilling description of a sadistic beating inflicted, for no apparent reason, on all the British officers. Yet Christmas was a special occasion, and Atholl and his fellow prisoners put everything they could into it.

Watching comrades die around him and suffering from malaria himself, he faced his first Christmas in captivity with gloom, then experienced some pleasant surprises:

Dec 23rd

Well, I guess this will prove the bluest Xmas I have had as there is next to nothing to eat, absolutely nothing to smoke either in the camp or village, nowhere to go and worst of all nobody to see. What wouldn't I do to get out of this lot! Weather still bitterly cold and still no fires. In fact, the whole bloody outlook stinks!!

Dec 24th

The Japs have promised us quite a few things for our Xmas and much to our surprise and delight kept their word. In the evening, the mine manager provided a gramophone and a good selection of records, Jazz and serious, to which we listened after supper when an issue of cigarettes and wine was made. When selections from Mozart and Beethoven were being played my thoughts went to home and I wondered how soon it would be before our reunion. All the Nips very affable during the concert and, in fact, we spent a most enjoyable evening.

Dec 25th

The food today has been marvellous! For breakfast we had barley porridge and sugar – we followed this up with bully sandwiches and cocoa in the forenoon – for lunch, pork, boiled spuds, cabbage and spaghetti whilst for supper, beef stew, roast spuds, beans, cabbage, duff with sugar sauce, and bread biscuits butter and wine. In the afternoon we were inspected by a Nip major and later had to move to our new quarters and, of course, I had to be orderly officer. In all, we had a far better Xmas than we ever dared hope for and I do feel the Japs did their best to give us a good time. A sing-song concert at night round the fire in the men's dining hall rounded off the best day of our captivity so far.

New Year's Eve was less positive:

Dec 31st

Everything very quiet today. Stayed in bed as my squitters had not improved. In the afternoon, the Japs started playing gramophone records and they had quite a good selection ranging from 'Lady of Spain' to 'Ave Maria'. In the evening quite a lot of fish, apples and oranges arrived but unfortunately most of the fish and oranges were rotten so the expected 'big eats' did not materialise. There was also an issue of sake and biscuits but the one thing that we really wanted i.e. cigarettes, failed to appear and the men were rather disgusted.

Stayed up to see in the New Year, the last person I saw in 1942 and the first I saw in 1943 was [his fiancée] Elizabeth as I looked at her photo during the change. Well, 1942 has been the most disastrous year in my sweet young life and I can only hope that the New Year will see the return of peace to this war-weary world, and that we

*can return to all those so near and dear to us, and find
them safe and well.*

That particular wish was not fulfilled. Christmas 1943 saw
Atholl still in captivity and the camp planning some lavish
entertainment:

Dec 22nd

*Very little doing all day, the only note-worthy event being
that Joe Kwiatkowski* [an American fellow-prisoner]
*managed to get some paper streamers which saved the day as
far as our Christmas decorations were concerned as...apart
from a rather futuristic Santa Claus on a sled with very
saucy reindeer and some evergreen surreptitiously removed
from the young trees in the camp, we had nothing with
which to relieve the grim and drab aspect of our room...*

Dec 25th

*Immediately after morning roll call, the room Xmas
committee got busy and prepared our half of the room for
our party: our bay was screened off by blankets, the tables
were covered with sheets, paper doilies were provided for
the plates, imitation candles and paper streamers providing
the table decorations along with the place cards. Just after
the meal had begun, old Tom came in, dressed up as Santa
Claus and distributed the presents to each member. When
the meal had finished the radio travelogue skit was put on,
the highlight of this being Lasher's Indian war dance which
was interrupted by the arrival of the guard commander*

who was more than startled to see a paint be-daubed face
peering at him round the door and a hand brandishing an
exceedingly murderous-looking cleaver just above it.

The arrival of Red Cross parcels added to the general feeling of good cheer, as did the fact that some of the inmates had managed to bribe the guards to bring them Japanese whisky.

Dec 26th

This evening in the canteen there was a performance of
'Ali Baba' which was without exception the funniest show
we have had yet, as contrary to Jap orders, costumes were
used and Hutch-Smith, Irwin and Pat Brougham dressed
up as robbers were absolute masterpieces; Gordon Eccles as
an usherette created quite a stir too.

Atholl ended 1943 on an optimistic note, convinced that victory and peace were in sight. But he had well over another year's imprisonment to endure, as the entry labelled 'Dec 28th 1944–Jan 10th 1945' reflected:

Well, a new year has begun and altho' I find that I am
quite unable to form any definite opinion as to when we
shall walk out of here free men, I am quite convinced
that it will come sometime during this year…most of us
have hacking coughs, the Japs are using the R/C cough
mixture to sweeten their tea and only issue a very small
quantity of diluted medicine in extreme cases… The folks
at home have featured a great deal in both my thoughts

*and dreams of late which does not tend to make one feel
contented with our present lot, but as I have said before,
'It can't be long now!'*

He had to wait until September – a month after the Japanese
surrender – but eventually his fortitude was rewarded.

John Fletcher-Cooke (later Sir John, CMG) was an
inmate of the same prison. His understated account makes
chilling reading. The work he mentions was hard labour,
underground, at the local dockyard, requiring the men to
rise at 5.30 a.m., start work at seven and visit the latrines
only during designated breaks – 'a serious hardship for those
suffering from dysentery':

We continued to work all through the Christmas
holidays. Christmas Eve was enlivened, not by Father
Christmas, but by some para-military organisation
of Japanese schoolboys who elected to hold their
nocturnal manoeuvres all round the camp. The
occasion was at least marked by noise, if not by carols.

On Christmas Day we were all weighed again.
I noticed that the two faces of the scales weighed
appreciably differently. I had dropped a few more
pounds. What was far more disturbing was the fact
that fifteen of the P.o.W.s now weighed considerably
less than fifty kilos.

Somehow or other Harry Radford had managed
to produce something that looked like Christmas
puddings. The guards ate them all....

The heavy snow which had fallen on a number of occasions during the preceding week lay thick on the ground. New Year's Day 1943 was the coldest we had, as yet, experienced.

Harry Radford had baked some oatmeal cakes to mark the occasion, but Nomoto [the camp commander] forbad their issue, saying that our digestions could not stand them. No doubt they suffered the same fate as the Christmas puddings.

The missionary Dr R Kenneth McAll and his wife Frances were interned in China by the Japanese. As their fourth Christmas approached, they wondered if they couldn't bring something of the spirit of Christmas to their twelve hundred fellow internees:

Together we studied the big disused warehouse which served us for dining-room and common-room. How could we decorate it? As a start, we set everyone collecting any bright-coloured stuff or objects that could be spared – match-boxes, silver paper, wrappings from tins. The walls of the room were huge and bare. Over each window hung Chinese matting, which served as blackout curtains. If we could paint pictures on the matting…? But, paint? We made black from soot, white from lime scraped from the sick-bay walls, and red from brick finely powdered. The ingredients were mixed up with rice-paste. With these paints and a brush made from old rope I set to work to cover the matting with Christmassy scenes.

So if you had come into the warehouse on Christmas Eve you would have pushed aside the sacking curtains and, slightly dazzled for a moment by the lights after the darkness outside, slightly repelled, perhaps, for a moment by the fuggy heat, you would have gazed at the multi-coloured decorations; at gay paper-chains made from paper wrappings from jam tins; at a huge, red, star-spangled bell in the middle of the room, made from a dressing gown and silver paper.

Then, glancing between the Oregon-pine pillars supporting the floor above, you would have seen, in bright red, black and white on the yellow mats, gay scenes of home. Snow-men, children tobogganing, carol-singers, Father Christmas with his reindeer, a child hanging up her stocking, an old-world inn and a stage-coach drawing up to it.

And, over there, on what had been the very biggest and blankest piece of wall, you would have seen the pièce de résistance – an old English fireplace. On the mantelshelf was a cluster of Christmas cards that people had made. Above was a sloping red-brick chimney-breast, with scroll and motto, and supporting the skull and antlers of a deer.

The fireplace had an astonishing effect on people. It wasn't removed after Christmas, and for the remainder of our stay in the camp people would sit round it and talk of their own firesides in far-away homes. Though it was only a painting, I sometimes saw men standing before it warming their seats...

During the evening we had a Christmas tableau. Half the camp came to see it, and filled the hall. Many people were moved to tears. Many of the Shanghai-landers knew nothing of Christmas until then. Other folk said it was the first time they had really celebrated Christmas. One woman, a captive in a freezing-cold Japanese prison, declared: 'This has been the happiest Christmas of my life.'

EPILOGUE

Prisoners of war may have faced 1945 with optimism, convinced that another year would see them home with their families. But back in the UK, that last Christmas of the war was one of contradictions. Informed opinion was that Germany was on the brink of defeat and that, as the song insisted, good times were just around the corner. The cover of the *Royal Army Service Corps Review for Xmas 1944* showed a jovial chef surrounded by smiling servicemen and bearing a Christmas pudding with the words 'Victory 1945' on it. Underneath was the caption 'Remember – it won't be long now!' Inside the magazine, the editorial contained this upbeat message:

This is our fourth Christmas, and we feel that our readers will not be disappointed with this year's issue and will find the magazine appropriately festive for a Christmas celebrated under happier auspices than for many years... We ourselves would like to wish you a Merry Christmas and a Happy New Year and that 1945 will bring many of you back to your homes to celebrate next Christmas at your own firesides.

Good Housekeeping's tone was also resolutely cheerful:

Christmas shopping is a little more promising this year. You can actually choose. And if there are still no electric trains, still no dolls with eyes that open and shut – well, who knows what next year may bring?

Advertisements, too, had become more optimistic: Moffat of Blackburn described their new electric cooker as 'well worth waiting for' and claimed that although 'supplies are limited at present owing to war requirements [...] we shall be ready to meet the post-war demand'. Phoenix, makers of clear glass ovenware, promised that 'the limited supplies of wartime would give place to the abundance of peace'. Even St Martin, manufacturers of chunky marmalade, looked forward to the day when 'there will be enough "CHUNKY" again to give all marmalade connoisseurs as much as they want'.

The year 1944 had, however, been a difficult one – for Londoners in particular. After an extended period of little or no bombing, the V-1s, or doodlebugs, had brought fear, death and destruction in a way that was all the more disheartening for coming when it did. The engines of these unmanned flying bombs made a distinctive puttering sound that gave them their other nickname of 'buzz bombs'; the noise ceased as the bombs went into a dive, meaning that silence was the most threatening sound of all. Doodlebugs often arrived before the warnings sounded – they were so fast that the sirens couldn't keep up. Once the engine cut out you had twelve seconds to take cover.

A second wave of evacuees left London to escape the onslaught. In July, a month after the first attacks, Vere Hodgson remarked, *'the atmosphere of London has changed. Back into the feeling of the Big Blitz. Apprehension in the air.'*

From September the V-1 was supplemented by the V-2, a guided ballistic missile popularly known as a Rocket. On New Year's Eve Vere noted fatalistically:

> *A few Rockets – but not near us. Frequently I wake up in the night and am surprised to find myself alive – because if you pass over with a Rocket Bomb you would never know until you came to – on the other side of life!*

The journalist Leonard Mosley, writing about London at the end of 1944, reflected what he perceived as a general gloom:

> Disillusionment and hopelessness were spectres at Christmas dinner all over the capital [...] No tinned fruits. No reduction of points on the purchase of the rarer foods. No oranges. No lemons...
>
> There was no doubt that this was the most miserable Christmas of the war. All the fine hopes of

the summer […] had faded. And with them, the spirit seemed suddenly to go out of Londoners. Five years of lowering diet, bombing, defeats and humiliations, conscription, the increasing regimentation and dim degradation of life in a great city in wartime seemed to have sapped the strength and optimism of seven million Cockneys.

One of Mosley's sources observed that everyone had been counting on the war being over by now and was feeling very flat because it wasn't: 'People are sick of the war. You can stand it so long but there comes a time when you can't stand it any more.' It's unlikely that the promise of abundant glass ovenware and chunky marmalade would have cheered these people up.

Victory did come, of course: in Europe in May 1945, and over the Japanese in August. Between those two landmark dates Winston Churchill's wartime government had been voted out of office and the lengthy task of rebuilding the country had begun. The shops weren't suddenly full of everything they had stocked before the war: shortages and food queues persisted; controls over food supplies actually became tighter. In 1947 even potatoes, which Potato Pete had promoted so assiduously, were rationed. Conditions gradually improved, but the last rationing wasn't abolished until 1954, nine years after the war ended. 'Post-war austerity' was a very real and depressing thing, and the habit of saving brown paper and string remained ingrained in many war survivors for the rest of their lives.

But even so, there was peace. The journalist and broadcaster Godfrey Winn, in New York for Christmas in 1945 to 'present a picture of a stricken Europe, still in a state of siege', noted that 'the opulence of Christmas in New York was savagely at variance with the pictures that crowded in my mind'. One of those pictures was encapsulated by a BBC broadcast he had made a few days earlier:

> ...of the most beautiful Christmas tree I have ever seen...in the Church of St-Martin-in-the-Fields. Every year it stands there, at the end of the nave, lit up, with the Star of Bethlehem touching its topmost branch, loaded down with presents, given by everyone...perhaps by you...for the children who have no parents, no address to which Father Christmas can come...
>
> I defy anyone to walk down that aisle on Christmas Eve, towards that great glow of coloured lights, and not understand what the message of Christmas really is, how Christmas belongs not only to the children, but to all of us who hold our hands to life, and are grateful to give, because of the overwhelming bounty we receive.

The Christmas tree, Winn observed, had special significance not only in London, but in New York too. One woman had said to him, 'It was not when the lights went full on in Broadway again, but when the Christmas trees were lit in Park Avenue, that I really believed the war was over.'

ACKNOWLEDGEMENTS

I don't think I've ever written a book that inspired more people to say, 'Oh, you must talk to my mother/aunt/ friend's uncle/sister's friend' and elicited more kindness and enthusiasm from friends, relations, casual acquaintances and complete strangers. Normally it's a polite exaggeration to say that 'this book couldn't have been written without the help of all these people', but in this case it is absolutely true.

So thanks first of all to Ann, Beryl and Norman, Brenda, Carol and John, Cec, Ellie, Felicity, the two Gills, Ginny and Geoff, Joe, Kathy, Jill, Julia and Peter, Liz, Lois, Lorraine, Niki, Pauline and Tony, Rebecca, Sheena, Sheila and Andy, Sheila and Dave, Ros and Sam, Ryan, Sue, Sue and Albert, Sue and Tony, and Tracey – all of whom facilitated, introduced, encouraged or reminisced – and to Ruth, who lent me her copy of *Christmas Lasts For Ever* and got me started.

The following also generously shared their memories or helped me to track down others who would:

Doreen Allan; Sheila Angeli; Roy Bartlett; Sheila Bellis; Joan Berry and her friends and relations in Woodbridge; Hazel Davey; Dai Charles and Nancy Evans; Jean Cock; Brenda Gordon; Biddy Guilford and Peter Fiennes; Kit Fleming; Rita Gibbs; June Harris; Dorothy Hayward; Rita Hayes; Shirley Hunter and her lunch club at Holy Trinity Church, Mildenhall; Stan Howe; Irvine Hunt; Brian Jackman; David Johnson; Aldwyn Jones; Mollie Kennedy; Yvonne Klarkowski; Mike Laxton; Bob Marshall; Gwen and Aneurin Morgan; David Parry; Joan Pype; Anita Setchfield; Dolly Sinden and the ladies of the Parish Church of the Holy Cross, Woodingdean; Audrey and Alec Sterrett; Kay Stewart and Elaine Stewart Knight; John Taranti; Nancy Titman; Jack Tring; Ronnie Walter; Valerie Warwick; Joan White; Wendy Winfield; and John Woodcock.

I have quoted extensively from private papers held in the Documents and Sound Section of the Imperial War Museum and am grateful to the friendly and efficient staff there, and to whoever designed the museum's wonderfully searchable website. The extracts on pages 3–5 and 54–7 are by James Cheeseman (Documents.15598, reproduced by permission of Mrs M Cheeseman); on page 41–4 by Viola Bawtree (Documents.1807, by permission of Bruce Gordon-Smith); on pages 101 and 191 by Mabel Harris (Documents.11882); page 108 by Bridget Elliott (Documents.25138, by permission of the author); pages 126–131 and 216–217 by Rose Cottrell (Documents.13128); pages 189–191 by Evelyn

ACKNOWLEDGEMENTS

and Ernest Harwood (Documents.16878, by permission of Michael Harwood); pages 233–4 by Stanley (known as Dan) Bridgen (Documents.22630, by permission of David Bridgen); pages 240–2 Lucy Addey (Documents.13229); page 242 Margaret Morgan (Documents.13863); pages 243 and 248–50 Eric Price (Documents.23865, by permission of John Price); page 244–5 Lt B F Spiller (Documents.11941); pages 246–7 Richard Legg (Documents.26272, by permission of the Imperial War Museum). Every effort has been made to contact the other copyright holders and, if they cared to contact me, I should be happy to acknowledge them in future editions.

My thanks also to Peter Grayson for permission to quote (page 74) from the life story of his aunt, Connie Ogdon, and to Ellie Lewis-Nunes and Sarah Lowry at Gunnersbury Park Museum for giving me access to their living history archive.

The extracts on pages 109, 157 and 174 are from the Foundling Voices oral history collection © The Foundling Museum – thanks to Alison Dukes, Collections Manager, for her generous help in sourcing these. I am grateful also to Colin Burgess for permission to quote (pages 255–6) from *The Diggers of Colditz* by Jack Champ and Colin Burgess; to Louise Reynolds for permission to quote (pages 261–4) from *Down to Bedrock* by Eric Cordingley; and Meg Parkes for extracts (pages 265–9) from her *Notify Alec Rattray…* and *A. A. Duncan Is OK*.

The reminiscence by an anonymous evacuee on pages 13–14 is from Ben Wicks's *No Time to Wave Goodbye* and is reprinted by permission of the author's estate and Bloomsbury

Publishing plc. The extracts from Vere Hodgson's diaries *Few Eggs and No Oranges* on pages 38–41 and 275 are reprinted by permission of Persephone Books Ltd.

The reminiscences by Helen Hardinge on pages 204–7, the anonymous nurse on pages 221–2, Dr Kenneth McAll on pages 270–2 and Godfrey Winn on pages 277 are taken from *Christmas Lasts For Ever*, compiled by Hannen Foss. The extract on pages 224–6 is from *The Maturing Sun* by Angela Bolton; pages 229–30 from *Valiant Quartet* by G G Connell; page 231 from *Fly for Your Life* by Larry Forrester; pages 232–3 from *Mediterranean Maelstrom* by G G Connell; pages 243–4 from *A Merchant Fleet in War* by Captain S W Roskill; pages 257–60 from *Prisoner of Hope* by David Wild. Publication details for these books are given in the Bibliography on page 283; again, efforts to trace copyright holders have been unsuccessful, but I should be happy to acknowledge them in future editions.

BIBLIOGRAPHY

Bartlett, Roy, *A Little Boy's War* (AuthorHouse, 2006)

Baybutt, Ron, *Camera in Colditz* (Hodder & Stoughton, 1982)

Bolton, Angela, *The Maturing Sun* (Imperial War Museum, 1986, and Headline Publishing Group, 1988)

Campbell, Clare, *Bonzo's War* (Constable, 2013)

Champ, Jack, and Burgess, Colin, *The Diggers of Colditz* (Orbis Publishing, 1985)

Connell, G G, *Mediterranean Maelstrom* (William Kimber, 1987)

Connell, G G, *Valiant Quartet* (William Kimber, 1979)

Cordingly, Eric, *Down to Bedrock* (Art Angels Publishing, 2013)

Fletcher-Cooke, Sir John, *The Emperor's Guest* (Hutchinson, 1971)

Forrester, Larry, *Fly for Your Life* (Frederick Muller, 1956)

Foss, Hannen, *Christmas Lasts For Ever* (Blandford/The Orion Publishing Group, 1946)

Fox, Barbara, *When the War Is Over* (Sphere, 2016)

Gardiner, Juliet, *The Children's War* (Portrait, in association with the Imperial War Museum, 2005)

Harris, June, *Andover's Wartime Years* (Andover History and Archaeology Society, 2001)

Hodgson, Vere, *Few Eggs and No Oranges: the Diaries of Vere Hodgson 1940–5* (Persephone Books, 1999; first published by Dennis Dobson, 1976)

McDowell, Colin, *Forties Fashion and the New Look* (Bloomsbury, 1997)

Merron, David, *Goodbye East End* (Corgi Books, 2015)

Moses, Anne and Brian, *Wartime Cookbook* (Wayland, 1995)

Mosley, Leonard, *Backs to the Wall* (Weidenfeld & Nicolson, 1971)

Parkes, Meg, *'Notify Alec Rattray…'* (Kranji Publications, 2002)

BIBLIOGRAPHY

Parkes, Meg, '...A. A. Duncan Is OK' (Kranji Publications, 2003)

Patten, Marguerite, We'll Eat Again (Hamlyn/Imperial War Museum, 1985)

Roskill, Captain S W, A Merchant Fleet in War (Alfred Holt, 1962)

Ross Collins, Stella, Christmas! (Kyle Cathie, 1999)

Summers, Julie, Jambusters (Simon & Schuster, 2013)

Wicks, Ben, No Time to Wave Goodbye (Bloomsbury, 1989)

Wicks, Ben, Waiting for the All Clear (Bloomsbury, 1990)

Wild, David, Prisoner of Hope (The Book Guild, 1992)